the girl's guide to

ACTION SPORTS

JESSICA EVELEIGH

A & C Black • London

First published in Great Britain 2009
by A&C Black Publishers Limited
36 Soho Square, London W1D 3QY
www.acblack.com

Copyright © Jessica Eveleigh, 2009

ISBN 978-0-7136-8942-6

A CIP catalogue record for this book is available from the British Library.

Cover and text designed by James Watson
Illustrations © Erica Sharp

This book is produced using paper that is made from wood grown in
managed, sustainable forests. It is natural, renewable and recyclable.
The logging and manufacturing processes conform to the environmental
regulations of the country of origin.

Printed in China by South China Printing Co.

ACKNOWLEDGEMENTS

Sara Burdon at Flowmtb, the July 2007 Dirt Girls, Louise Alexander at Mountaingirl, Milly Hawkins and Robin Mannering at Custom Breaks, Ruth Martin at Mudunlimited, Helen Lavender at rudechalets, Tammy Esten at Mint Snowboarding, Jon Finch at Loose Fit Surf Shop, Jon Price at Big Blue Surf School, Ben Freeston at Magic Seaweed, Mark Bessell at Geronimo Sports, Jane Bentley at Cardiff University, Mandy Richards at Escape Adventures NZ, Tony Butt and Paul Russell at the University of Plymouth, Tina Gardner at the British Mountaineering Council, Diddy aka Sara Sturrock, Catherine Gordon, Pauline Adams, Tim Rogers, Lucy Darkin, Jayne Kerridge, Pearl Howie, Jade and Leah Andrews, Hannah Wilson, Tammy Osborne, Faye Page, Roslyn Cassidy, Belinda Baggs.

Robert Foss, Lucy Beevor, Kate Burkhalter and Charlotte Croft at A&C Black.

Erica Sharp for her beautiful illustrations.

Neil Adams for the oceanic depths of your love, support and encouragement.

My family for your spirit, determination and sense of adventure.

contents

INTRODUCTION

There are so many things that we are able to do, but sometimes we are held back by our own silly notions of what we can or can't do. Often it's because we perceive that the people who are already doing what we want to do are in some way superior – cooler, fitter, more knowledgeable, experienced, confident, gutsy, or whatever. What's easy to forget, though, is that everyone was a beginner once and may have had the same fears that are holding you back. What's more, there's no doubt they've made endless mistakes to get to where they are today. But, the only mistake they didn't make was to begin in the first place.

Action sports are often dubbed 'extreme' or 'adrenalin' sports, which implies they're inherently laced with risk. This is one reason women are often put off by the sports covered in this book: adventure racing, climbing, mountain biking, snowboarding and surfing. Yet, they're only extreme if you take extremely stupid risks – attempt a black run on your second day of snowboarding, say, or go out in 30-foot surf after just a few lessons. As long as you're aware of your own level and ability, and respect the environment around you, then you'll only ever push yourself just outside your comfort zone, never into danger.

Another reason is that these sports can often come across as cliquey, with their own language and fashion. As soon as you dip below the surface, however, you'll realise that it's only jargon and it's easy to pick up the terminology. Meanwhile, the fashion is practical as much as anything. Still, there's no doubt that having to ask stupid questions can be a limiting factor – certainly, no one enjoys being green. So, that's why you're reading *The Girl's Guide to Action Sports*.

In each chapter, you'll find the answers to those questions (which aren't stupid, by the way). You'll learn a bit about what the sport is, its history, its body-and-mind benefits and everything you need to get started. There's even a breakdown of the essential gear and explanations of the fundamental techniques, plus travel tips if you've been inspired to go global with your new-found passion.

Armed with this knowledge, you've every excuse to get going. But, if for some strange reason you do need further persuading, here are the returns you'll get for your effort. For starters, unlike going to the gym or sessions with that expensive personal trainer, both of which rely on external sources of motivation and reward to keep you on track, action sports have an intrinsic value. That is, the more you do them, the more they become part of your personality – 'It's who I am and what I do.' OK, so you may need a little coaxing out of bed for a dawn surf on a winter's morning or an afternoon's mountain biking in the pouring rain, but once you're out there you'll quickly remember why you love it. Getting fit will be a happy side effect rather than the main goal.

While you're keeping your body in check, you'll also be giving your mind a thorough workout. There's no doubt that doing action sports can be life-enhancing. Every minute brings with it the potential for achievement and, with your mind focussed on the moment, learning and perfecting new skills, you'll find that your self-assurance and sense of determination grows without you even realising. This can only have a positive impact on other areas of your life – action sports provide an exhilarating means of escaping from the stresses of daily life, and they give you the confidence to deal with them too.

Although essentially individual pursuits – which means you can improve at your own pace – adventure racing, climbing, mountain biking, snowboarding and surfing are intensely social sports. Through them you'll make friends who will give you the support and motivation you need to continue and progress. Action sports heighten both good and bad emotions, bring them to the surface and enable people to share and build on them. This opportunity for openness and honesty – not to mention the times when you may have to trust others with your safety – is the metal that will forge friendships for life. When everyone else is stuck inside watching TV, you'll be outside together having all the fun in the world.

Which brings us to the outdoors. The last, but certainly not the least, reward is the benefit of exercising among the elements. Research shows that being surrounded by nature can improve your mental wellbeing, have a positive effect on your mood, and boost your self-esteem. It can also inspire spiritual feelings of 'being at one' with yourself and the environment. So, there you go. Action sports are not just about your body, they're about the mind and the soul too. That leaves one final stupid question to answer: What are you waiting for? Enjoy.

THE GIRL'S GUIDE TO
ADVENTURE RACING

WHAT IS IT?

An adventure race is a multi-sport endurance event that typically involves running, mountain biking, navigating, kayaking and team challenges. A race can last anything between three and six hours for entry-level events, to 11 or more days for an expedition-style race. Traditionally the terrain is off-road and through wilderness, but there are now a number of urban-based events.

The exact format varies from race to race and the course usually remains a secret until hours, or sometimes just minutes, before the start. Competitors must navigate their way to as many checkpoints as they can to accumulate the maximum number of points while aiming to finish fastest, and before the official cut-off time.

BODY AND MIND BENEFITS

Signing up for an adventure race provides the ultimate fitness goal, and one that will benefit both body and mind, testing your physical and mental endurance. Training is the best excuse to try new sports, such as off-road running, mountain biking, kayaking, climbing and rope skills, with other up-for-it girls – or boys. In fact, the social side of adventure racing (AR) is one of its greatest appeals. Competing together will forge unique bonds between you and your teammates and help you understand your personal strengths and weaknesses. Meanwhile, switching between the different disciplines conditions every muscle group in your body which, as long as you're sensible and don't take risks, means you can work hard without the worry of injury.

HOW IT ALL BEGAN

In 1994 fledgling American sports journalist Martin Dugard coined the term 'adventure racing' while previewing the infamous Raid Gauloises, which took place that year on the jungle-dense island of Borneo. The corporate desk slave turned freelance writer was making a career for himself covering this expedition-style, multi-sport event which had been designed by Frenchman Gerard Fusil to push even the toughest athletes to their limits.

Sadly the Raid Gauloises is no more. Nor is the epic Eco Challenge created by one-time Raider Mark Burnett as the American rival to Fusil's iconic race. Nevertheless, other equally formidable events are still going strong. New Zealand's Southern Traverse and the Speight Coast to Coast, along with Primal Quest in the US, still represent the ultimate ambitions of adventure racers around the globe.

However, you don't have to travel to far-flung places to take part. The UK is one of the top destinations in the world for one- and two-day entry-level to intermediate AR, while Europe often hosts longer, multi-day events.

Women have always played an important part in AR. In the early years of the sport, most events stipulated mixed teams of up to five members, while many now allow single-sex teams and elite pairs. Recently, there has been a surge of women pursuing AR, which has given rise to all-female squads in the UK and Europe.

GETTING STARTED

ENTRY-LEVEL RACES
There are numerous AR events specifically aimed at novices, or which have entry categories for both novices and masters. These take place throughout the year,

but tend to be more frequent in autumn and winter since other athletes, such as runners, triathletes and mountain bikers, use them to add spice to their out-of-season training.

Entry-level races are specifically designed with fun in mind. They provide an introduction to the sport, and the courses are challenging yet realistic for beginners to complete.

Most entry-level events last between three and five hours. Some may get you navigating from the beginning, others will pre-mark the route for you to make life easier. All involve some off-road running and mountain biking, others will also include kayaking as the third main discipline.

There's no need to rush through your progression from entry-level to one- or two-day races, though, as the more experienced you become in these, the more prepared you'll be for the next step.

ONE-DAY RACES
Like entry-level races, one-day races typically last three to five hours. However, the courses are not specifically aimed at beginners and will challenge most competitors, whatever their level of experience or fitness. Indeed, course designers will often set courses that are just possible for the most experienced athletes to finish in around two and a half or three hours.

You'll almost certainly be expected to devise and follow your own route around the course, although there may be suggested short cuts to enable slower teams to complete the event within the official cut-off time. There's unlikely to be extra time for rest and transition between disciplines and you'll be racing non-stop from start to finish.

TWO-DAY RACES
The next step up from one-day races, two-day races could involve a three-hour prologue on the first day, followed by a 10-hour race on the second day. Or, it could take the form of a 24- or 30-hour endurance race that goes through the night and during which you decide when to rest or sleep.

FINDING A TEAM

Training and competing in a team is at the heart of AR. The standard team size is three, but it can be as few as two or as many as five. Try competing in mixed- and women-only teams as you'll gain a great deal from both experiences.

Team members don't have to be your best mates, although they may quickly become some of your most trusted friends. You can recruit fellow action girls or guys through your local running, mountain biking, triathlon, climbing or kayaking clubs, or at your workplace. Race organisers can often put you in touch with other people in your area looking for teammates, too.

Two things are vitally important however: firstly, teammates must be in it for the same reason, whether that's simply to have a laugh and complete, or to race like demons and compete; secondly, you must train with your teammates.

Girls who... Adventure race

Kirsty Maguire, 28, Architect
'AR is a real challenge. Everyone enjoys pushing their own boundaries, discovering what their strengths are – both as individuals and as a team. And, if you make training fun, then it's easy to get out for a run or three-hour mountain bike. Being around like-minded people is the ultimate motivation.'

SUPPORT CREW

Whether it's your best friend, sibling, partner or parents, it's a good idea to enlist some kind of support crew. Their role may be as simple as driving you to and from the event, which will conserve precious energy pre-race and ensure that you're not driving in a dangerous, bleary-eyed state on the way home. However, if they're willing, you may also want them to prepare your pre-race dinner, breakfast on the morning of the event and a slap-up meal for you to tuck into shortly after crossing the finish line. The extra hands will also come in handy when you're packing and unloading kit.

RACE PREPARATION

In the week before the race, eat well, sleep well and back off the training – don't do more than one or two light sessions. Use the time you've freed up to ensure that you have everything you need on the kit list (see opposite). Work out how you're going to get to and from the event and make sure everyone, including your support crew, knows who's doing what.

RACE DAY

Arrive with plenty of time to unpack your gear, register, pick up hire equipment, go through any mandatory kit and medical checks, get acquainted with the race schedule, go over your race strategies, pose for photographs, check out the event area and meet the (friendly) competition. Then, the only thing left to do is race!

EATING ON THE GO

Nutrition is crucial in AR. You need to have energy throughout the race as well as at the finish. Try these top five on-the-go snacks – and remember to drink plenty of water.

- energy gels – look for ones made with natural ingredients such as honey
- energy bars – brands such as the SIS Go bar are made with fruit and one bar counts towards two of your daily fruit quota
- peanut butter and jam sandwich on wholegrain bread – the perfect sugar, protein and carb combo

- a couple of slices of fruit malt loaf
- fruit and nut flapjack.

RECOVERY

You're going to be tired when you finish. Eat well, get home safely, do some stretching, and sleep. If you're racing on a Sunday or over a whole weekend, take the Monday off work as it can take a while for the adrenalin of the event to wear off enough for you to get a decent night's kip. Forget about training the following week. Rest up and use the time to reflect on the race. Ask yourself questions such as: What were the highlights? Low points? What did you do well? How could you have done better? What were your team's strengths? What would you do differently next time?

GEAR GUIDE

KIT LISTS

Every AR event will outline a mandatory kit list in the race details. There may be team and individual kit lists. You must have everything on the mandatory kit lists, otherwise you won't be able to compete. As well as kit checks at registration, there may be spot checks during the race aimed at catching out competitors who've been tempted to ditch some weight from their packs in transition.

As well as mandatory kit lists, race organisers may also recommend that teams and individuals carry additional pieces of kit. Don't overlook these, as they are for competitors' benefit. When you sign up for a race, make sure that you're familiar with both. Give yourself plenty of time to buy or borrow everything you need and get used to carrying and using your gear during training.

RACE-SPECIFIC KIT

Race organisers usually provide you with additional essential kit. This could include a *kayak, buoyancy aid, race map, electronic scoring device* to record your checkpoint visits and times, and *race numbers*. Anything else, such as *climbing and kayaking helmets*, can usually be hired.

FOOTWEAR

For AR you'll need a pair of *off-road running, AR* or *trail shoes* that are supportive, protective, lightweight and fast-draining as your feet will get soggy and dirty. These should see you through every challenge.

If you use *SPDs* (see p70) on your mountain bike, make sure you have a sturdy pair of bike shoes that you'll be comfortable walking in should you need to get off your bike and carry it at any point. To save time in transition, practise changing in and out of your trail and bike shoes before the race.

SOCKS

Invest in two or three pairs of supportive *running socks*. As well as providing support in key areas such as the heel and toe, they can also help prevent blisters. Alternatively, you could use thick walking socks or double-up on two pairs of ordinary socks.

CLOTHING

Although it can be expensive, there's no doubt that wearing the right technical apparel will help you cope with all the mud, sweat and tears of AR. A pair of *padded cycling shorts* or *tights* will make the hours spent in the saddle much more comfortable. To save time in transition, go for a tight fitting pair that will be comfortable and lightweight enough for running, climbing and kayaking. Alternatively, wear a pair of supportive, lightweight running shorts or tights for the other disciplines and change into your cycling shorts/tights for the bike leg as padding can feel unpleasant when wet.

The key to dressing your top half is layers. Most technical apparel is lightweight and designed to pack down tightly, so always pack one or two more layers than you think you'll need. Wear a *supportive sports bra* underneath a *wicking vest* or *T-shirt* that is made from a technical material designed to 'wick' away sweat and moisture from your skin. Then comes a merino wool or synthetic *base layer*. These are available in different weights, so wear one suited to the conditions.

Depending on the weather you may want to pull an insulating *fleece* over this. Finally, finish everything off with a breathable *water and windproof jacket*, plus a *hat* and *gloves*. *Bike gloves* with a suede palm will protect your hands from falls on the bike and can also be used for rope work.

BACKPACK

In an entry-level race it's unlikely that you'll have to carry all your kit throughout the race. However, you'll definitely need to carry items such as food, pens, a whistle, mobile phone and water. Buy the smallest pack you can get away with. Some have straps, expandable mesh sections and bungy-ropes that will keep extra kit secure on the outside of the pack.

Make sure it has straps across the chest and around the waist, as this distributes the weight more evenly across your back, shoulders and hips, and think about getting one that can accommodate a hydration pack (see below). Women-specific backpacks are available.

HYDRATION SYSTEM

Keeping well-hydrated is crucial. *Water bottles* are fine for carrying fluids, but they can be cumbersome and will add seconds to your finishing time as you have to stop each time you want a drink. So, you need a more efficient solution.

Firstly, fix a *bottle cage* to your mountain bike for a *sports bottle* with a nozzle that's easy to drink from. These usually carry about 500ml to 750ml of fluid and you may want to make up an energy drink to go in this. To carry the bulk of your fluids, however, you're best off with a *hydration pack*, which typically holds around 1.5 to 2 litres. These plastic 'bladders' are designed to slide into the rear compartment of a backpack. A tube extends from the bladder, with a locking valve on one end that allows you to drink while you're on the move. Problem solved. Avoid filling your hydration pack with energy drinks as firstly, you'll feel queasy if you have too much, and, secondly, they clog up the bladder and valve.

COMPASS

Compasses feature on most mandatory kit lists. In an entry-level race where the navigation is relatively simple you'll need one to at least check you're heading in the right direction. In some events, one of the team challenges may be orienteering. You don't need an all-singing, all-dancing compass, just a basic one that can be used on map scales 1:50,000 and 1:25,000.

WRITING TOOLS
You'll need a *pencil, rubber, permanent marker* and a couple of different *coloured highlighter pens* to mark up checkpoints and to plan your route. Keep them in a watertight bag – a ziplock food bag does the job.

NOTEPAD
Carry a *notepad* to scribble on when planning your route, to record any last-minute briefings from race organisers and to take notes while completing a challenge. Stow it in the watertight bag with your pens.

WHISTLE
Keep a *whistle* on you for use in case of emergency. Make sure it's easily accessible.

HEAD TORCH
A *head torch* is essential for night navigation and handy too if you have to scramble down a dark tunnel.

FIRST AID KIT
Carry a *first aid kit* with you at all times. Buy a ready-made one or make up your own. Don't forget to include arnica cream for bumps and bruises. Keep it in a watertight container.

MOUNTAIN BIKE (MTB)
Invest in the best *mountain bike* that you can afford. It will pay off during training and racing. For AR, a cross-country hardtail MTB with front suspension forks and disc brakes is ideal.

Shop around and try various makes and frame sizes until you find the bike you're most comfortable riding. Ask someone experienced to help you set your bike up correctly, too, as this will make all the difference to your riding experience.

Keep your bike clean and well maintained and learn how to do basic emergency repairs. For more on MTBs, see p66.

MTB SOS
Always carry a *spare inner tube, puncture repair kit, pump* and basic *bike multi-tool* when out training and on race day.

MTB ACCESSORIES
A *cycling helmet* is essential. Get one with ventilation that fits well. You may also need a *bell* to alert other path and trail users of your presence, and *lights* if you're going to be doing any riding after dusk. A *map mount* is useful for navigating. You could buy one or make your own from a square of an old plastic 'For sale' sign secured to your bike with plastic zip ties.

CANOES AND KAYAKS
You'll come across three basic types of watercraft. A *canoe* is an open-top boat in which the canoeist traditionally kneels and uses a *single-blade paddle*. More common is a *kayak* with a *double-blade paddle*. The kayaker sits inside the kayak or on a raised deck depending on the style of kayak. Race organisers often use *inflatable kayaks*.

You won't normally be expected to buy your own canoe or kayak in an entry-level race – check the event details to find out which type you'll be paddling and get experience of handling one in training. *Buoyancy aids* and *helmets* should also be available from race organisers.

CLIMBING/ROPE WORK EQUIPMENT
Unless race organisers specifically state that you need climbing shoes, a pair of grippy *off-road running shoes* should suffice. These will be more than adequate for most rope work, including rope ladders and cargo nets, abseiling and zip wires. To protect your hands, wear your bike gloves or a pair of leather/suede gardening gloves.

A *climbing harness* is essential for all rope work. Although you can often hire climbing harnesses from race organisers, if you're planning on doing a number

of events get your own. Buy a new harness, never secondhand and make sure it fits well. You'll also need a *carabiner* device and a *climbing helmet*. For more on climbing gear, see p35.

BEAUTY SPOT

Even if you're covered in mud, you'll want to look your best for photographs. Practise different ways of wearing your hair that'll work while you're running, as well as underneath safety helmets for biking, kayaking and climbing. Opt for a style that won't need adjusting in transition, either. Try bunches. They may be girly, but they look cute and stay put.

BASIC TECHNIQUES

RUNNING

You don't need to be an ultra-fast runner for AR. Navigation skills are more important than running ability, so that you're always en route for your next checkpoint. However, you do need experience of running off-road, so make sure you regularly hit the trails during your training.

Team running strategies include: towing (literally, with a towline made from a piece of rope) or pushing (with a light hand on their back) slower teammates; agreeing to walk up hills, jogging on the flat and running fast downhill; or setting intervals, such as walking at a fast pace for five minutes, then running at a steady pace for 10 minutes.

Whatever strategy you decide, it is important that you stick together. Race rules usually state that team members should be within 10 to 25 metres of each other at all times, but it can be demoralising if one teammate is continually left behind. So, keep your team moving at an equal pace, with everyone on an equal footing.

MOUNTAIN BIKING

As with running, you need to gain experience of going off-road. It's crucial to hone your MTB handling skills and to build up endurance. Practise correct *gear selection*; riding over *roots*, *rocks* and other *obstacles*; doing *drop offs*; *ascending*; *descending*; taking *corners*; tackling *switchbacks*; and other technical skills. For more on this, see p75.

To build your confidence, you can *session* a particular skill. For instance, if you're nervous about drop offs (cycling down a 'step' in the trail), then find a smallish one and practise it over and over again until you're comfortable with it. Then move onto a bigger drop and repeat the process.

It's important to be confident, too. Pick a line down the trail, stick to it and keep up your speed – trust that your bike can tackle anything you throw at it. If you slow to a wobble you're likely to topple over.

Get out with your teammates as often as possible. In the early days, you may want the fastest or most experienced biker to take the lead. This will force other team members to keep up their pace as they follow the leader's line along the trail. As other team members become more confident, take turns at the front.

Nightriding is a brilliant way of developing your skills and confidence. Hire or invest in a powerful pair of nightlights (see p72) and hit your local trails. Even the most familiar tracks will take on a whole new dimension under the cover of darkness.

When racing, you can use similar team strategies to running, including towing and pushing. Agree on your MTB strategies beforehand and practise them in training. And, don't forget, good navigation is also essential.

NAVIGATION

To be truly successful at AR, you need to have sharp navigation skills. But don't worry if you can't tell your eastings from your northings yet. Practise your map reading skills as much as you can and be prepared to make mistakes while training and racing.

To get your brain into gear, study maps of your local area and plan your own running and biking routes. Also keep an eye out for introductory *orienteering* events organised through your local club. These are a fun, hands-on way of picking up the basics, especially if you're not familiar with using a compass.

Maps are 2-D representations of the 3-D landscape, which enable you to visualise what a place looks like and to work out where you're going. To create this representation, maps use *symbols* for features such as churches, pubs, minor roads, footpaths and bridleways. Start by familiarising yourself with the various symbols on the map key.

To represent *distance*, maps are drawn to scale. The most common scales in Europe are: 1:25,000, for which one centimetre on the map is equivalent to 250 metres on the ground; and 1:50,000, for which one centimetre on the map is equivalent to 500 metres on the ground.

To make things easier, maps are also drawn on a *grid*. On a 1:25,000 scale map, grid squares are four centimetres apart. On a 1:50,000 map squares are two centimetres apart. For both scales, each grid square represents one kilometre by one kilometre on the ground.

Gradients are shown using *contour lines*. These are the pink squiggly lines that you can see all over a map. The closer together the contour lines, the steeper the gradient. The numbers on the contour lines indicate height and are usually given at 10-metre vertical intervals.

To indicate direction, maps show north, south, east and west. North is always shown on the map and is usually at the top. To confuse things, there's a *magnetic north* and a *grid north*. Depending on which country you're in, the two norths may vary by a few degrees. However, if there's only a small variation, such as three degrees for the UK, then it's fine to use grid north without any correction.

To pinpoint a location such as an AR checkpoint, you can use a numerical *grid reference* using the *grid lines*. The vertical grid lines are called *eastings* and the horizontal grid lines are called *northings*.

The simplest grid reference is a *four figure grid reference* which is a quick way to identify any box on the map. To make the location even more specific you can further sub-divide the box by 10 to enable you to give a *six figure grid reference*. You give eastings first, then northings. To remember this use the phrase: 'go along the corridor and then up the stairs.'

There are two main techniques you can use to check that you're going in the right direction: the first, and most useful, is *orienting the map*; the second is *taking a bearing*.

BASIC COMPASS SKILLS

Orienting the map
1   Place your compass flat on the map.
2   Rotate the map until the north on the map is aligned with the north on the *compass needle*.
3   The map is now oriented to the terrain. You can now use *feature recognition* to check your position and determine your direction.

Taking a bearing
1   Using your compass, align the long edge of the *baseplate* with the starting point and the destination on your map. The *direction of travel arrow* should be facing towards the destination.
2   Place the compass on the map and turn the *rotating housing* until the *north alignment* arrow on the bottom of the capsule is in line with north on the map.
3   Hold the compass in your hand in front of you, with the direction arrow pointing straight ahead. Rotate your body until the north on the *compass needle* lines up with the north arrow on the bottom of the capsule. The direction arrow is now pointing in the direction that you want to travel.

To identify where you are on the map and where you want to go, you can use *feature recognition*. You can identify a wide range of features on the map using the key. These include: *water, rock and vegetation* features; *man-made* features, for instance, electricity pylons and water towers; and, roads, paths, bridleways and other *linear* features. You can also use the contour lines on the map to identify different *land forms*, such as mountains, peaks, hills, knolls, valleys, ridges and plateaus.

On foot, you can estimate distances by *pace counting*, which is a skill that you should practise repeatedly in training. It involves counting the number of paces it takes you to cover a set distance, 100 metres for example, over different kinds of terrain. Alternatively, when running or on the bike, you could time how long it takes you to cover a certain distance. Once you have a good idea of your pacing and timing, you can use these techniques during a race for accurate navigation. You may find it's easiest for one team member to estimate the distance you've travelled, while another checks off features on the map. Distance estimation is particularly useful for night navigation.

Getting between checkpoints in the fastest time possible is key to AR. When planning your route, take the route that is the safest and easiest to navigate. Don't always opt for the most direct route, either. For instance, it may be better to skirt around the bottom of a hill rather than waste valuable energy climbing steep gradients.

CANOEING AND KAYAKING

Before you get in a boat, you should be able to swim at least 50 metres in a buoyancy aid, preferably further. Ideally, you should also take some kayaking lessons at your nearest watersports centre or join in with your local club.

Sitting in a canoe or kayak, keep a straight, relaxed posture. Lean slightly forward – if you lean back it will put too much weight on the back of the boat. Whether you're using a single-blade paddle in a canoe or a double-blade paddle in a kayak, aim to develop an *efficient stroke*. Reach forward with the paddle and slip the entire blade into the water before pulling back. Keep your arms straight and rotate your body as you pull into the stroke and snap the paddle out of the water as soon as it's parallel with your waist. Use the strong muscles in your back rather than the weaker muscles in your arms. If there are two of you in the boat, the person at the front should set the *paddling rhythm* while the person at the back acts as *helmsman* with responsibility for *steering*.

ROPE SKILLS
While it's a good idea to have a bit of experience of climbing (see p29), the main rope skills you're likely to need for AR are *abseiling* (descending on ropes, also called *rappelling*), climbing *rope ladders*, scrambling over *cargo nets* and negotiating *zip lines* (also known as death slides).

For abseiling, make sure you get some professional lessons in advance of the race. To practise the other skills, find out about army-style assault courses and rope adventure centres that are open to the public.

MENTAL SKILLS
AR takes brains not just brawn. The ability to make quick decisions, delegate, be diplomatic, and to know when it's time to lead and when it's time to be led, are all essential skills. When the pressure is on, remember the following:

- *Keep focused* At the start of the race, ignore other teams and stay focused on your race strategy. Don't get carried away by adrenalin and speed off without proper planning. When you start to get tired, make sure you're switched on and maintain focus.
- *Stay calm* If you get lost while navigating, stay calm and don't get cross with the navigator. Slow down and retrace your steps if you need to.
- *Recognise it will get hard* Expect it, embrace it and recognise that this is why you're doing the event. Focus on the situation and acknowledge the fact you're handling it well.
- *Stay upbeat* When the race gets tough, stay upbeat. A simple smile can make a huge difference.

TEAM WORK
Ensure that everyone in your team has a role and that they stick to it. It's preferable for the navigator to be relatively strong. Let them go to the front

and, if they're flagging, carry their kit. Don't distract the navigator, as they'll lose concentration.

Everyone should do their best to avoid doing things that will irritate others. Most teams will have arguments within their ranks at some point, especially when they're tired. Try to avoid arguments but accept they will happen. Agree that no one will bear grudges and that each time you finish a particular section of the race the slate will be wiped clean. Above all, however, remember to enjoy the experience.

Girls who... Adventure race

Caroline Wallace, 29, PE teacher

'I love the mystery and excitement of adventure racing. One minute you'll be climbing, then kayaking, then abseiling off a cliff face. You often don't know what you're going to be doing until minutes before – that means you have to learn how to make very quick decisions.'

TAKING IT FURTHER

If you've got the AR bug, then it won't be long before you're dreaming of doing an expedition-style event. These can last up to around 11 days and take you through some of the world's most breathtaking regions of wilderness. However, you'll need to have competed at quite a high level in the shorter adventure races before you enter and will need to raise considerable cash and sponsorship for the trip to cover gear, travel and entry fees. But don't let that put you off. It will certainly be one of the most amazing experiences of your life.

AR FIT

TRAINING TACTICS

Each team member will have different strengths and weaknesses. During training, it can be tempting to favour the discipline in which you have the most competence. However, this is unlikely to improve your overall enjoyment of the race. The best tactic, therefore, is to train to your weaknesses and race to your strengths. The two key fitness disciplines are running and mountain biking. So, if you're a strong runner, put in extra effort on the biking, and vice versa.

TRAINING SCHEDULE

To ensure that you've got everything covered for AR, it can be very helpful to devise a training schedule. Beginners should aim for around eight hours each week. Shorter, regular sessions are better than longer, intermittent periods of training. It may therefore be easier to break up your training into different mini-sessions spread throughout the day. For example, bike to work, run in your lunch break and do some stretches for flexibility or strength and core training exercises when you get home. Remember to take at least one rest day a week.

You needn't do all of your training sessions together as a team, as it may not be practical. But do make sure that you get together at least once a week for a bike or run. For the other disciplines – navigation, kayaking and rope skills – you should aim for at least one training session in each, every month. Make these a fun group activity at weekends.

BEGINNER AR WEEKLY TRAINING SCHEDULE

Below is an example of a typical beginner's weekly training schedule for AR.
Use this as a framework for building your own schedule.

Monday	30min run; 30min bike
Tuesday	30min run; 30min flexibility
Wednesday	1hr bike
Thursday	1hr navigation walk
Friday	rest day
Saturday	2hr team bike ride; 1hr rope or kayaking skills
Sunday	1.5hr team run and bike 'brick' session; 30min flexibility.

RUNNING

Much of the running in AR is off-road. Running down trails and forest tracks, through mud and across country requires more balance and agility than road running. Make at least one of your weekly training runs an off-road run of five-plus miles, keeping the pace steady and varying the terrain and gradient as much as possible.

BIKING

While biking to work or around town will build up your endurance, you also need to practise your off-road handling skills. A two- to three-hour MTB session is the perfect excuse to get out and explore the countryside near where you live. (For more on getting bike fit, see p79.)

TRANSITIONS

When you've put so much effort into racing hard, the last thing you want to do is lose valuable time in transition. Work out a system for keeping your kit organised, so everything you may need for the different stages of the race is easily accessible, and practise changing in and out of your kit with speed.

You also need to get your body used to running off the bike, and biking after a run, so that your muscles don't turn to jelly on race day. Do this in training by regularly splitting sessions between the two. For instance, run for 30 minutes, then bike for 30 minutes. Triathletes have nicknamed this a 'brick' session.

KAYAK

To get paddle fit, you need to develop upper body strength, as well your core, abdominal and back strength – all of which will benefit the other disciplines. Join a regular circuit training class or do your own circuit at home, including crunches, press ups, squats, bicep curls, back extensions and balances on a Swiss (stability) ball. Include one kayaking session in your training schedule each month.

ROPE SKILLS

Building your aerobic fitness through biking and running will prepare you well for rope skills, such as scrambling cargo nets and climbing rope ladders, while regular strength and core conditioning will help develop muscles you need for climbing. (For more tips on climbing fitness, see p50.) Include one session at an indoor climbing wall, assault course or rope adventure centre in your training schedule each month.

FLEXIBILITY

Improving your flexibility will help prevent injury and ensure that your muscles are working efficiently. Make sure you regularly stretch all the major muscle groups, including your quads, hamstrings, hip flexors, back, chest and arms.

AR TRAVEL

DECIDING WHERE AND WHEN TO GO

The most comprehensive source of AR information on the web is www.sleepmonsters.com. It includes race calendars for events around the world. So, if you've tried a few events on your home turf and are tempted to travel further afield, this is the place to find out what's happening when and where in the AR world.

TRAVELLING BY PLANE
When booking your flight, check the luggage allowances and the airline's policy on carrying sports equipment to avoid levying any additional costs at the airport.

PACKING YOUR KIT
When packing your kit you need to be organised. Write a list of every item you'll need, including everything on the mandatory and recommended kit lists. But don't go over the top and pack unnecessary additional kit 'just in case'.

If you're travelling to the event by car, pack all your race gear in transparent, clearly-labelled plastic boxes. For air travel, take your race pack on as hand luggage and pack everything else into a hardwearing duffle bag. To keep things organised, use sturdy pieces of cardboard to compartmentalise your duffle bag. For tips on packing your MTB, see p81.

TOP FIVE ADVENTURE RACES FOR BEGINNERS

ACE Races
Questars
Helly Hansen Adventure Series
Rat Race
Dynamic Adventure Racing

FIND OUT MORE

www.sleepmonsters.com
The home of the international AR community on the web.

IF YOU LIKE ADVENTURE RACING, TRY...

Off-road triathlon
Orienteering
Mountain bike orienteering.

JARGON BUSTER

Checkpoint Registration points at specific points on the course that teams must visit during the race. Some checkpoints are obligatory, others are optional

Cut-off time The maximum amount of time that competitors are given to complete the race

Feature recognition Using symbols on a map to navigate your way on the ground

Grid reference A four- or six-figure number that indicates a specific point on a map

Mandatory kit Essential gear that you must have to enter the race

Rope skills Any activity that involves ropes, such as climbing, abseiling or rappelling, zip wires and cargo nets

Route planning Working out the quickest, safest and most efficient way of getting around the race course

Stages The different sections of the race, such as running, biking and kayaking

Team challenges Physical and mental tasks designed to test competitors at various stages of the event and enable them to collect more race points

Transition area Place where you leave kit needed for different stages of the race.

THE GIRL'S GUIDE TO
CLIMBING

02

WHAT IS IT?

The aim of climbing is to get from A to B across a boulder or rock face in a series of moves that require balance, coordination and problem solving skills. There's no single environment for climbing. One day you might be scrambling up a 5-metre high artificial wall at an indoor climbing centre, another day you might be bouldering just a metre above the ground on the moors. Then, as you become more experienced, you could easily be scaling a 10 metre plus rock face outdoors with the sea crashing below, or with breathtaking vistas of the mountains all around you. Like many action sports, on one level, climbing is essentially an individual pursuit. However, communication, trust and friendship are also fundamental to the sport – climbers work in pairs, each ensuring the safety of the other, whether that's spotting their partner while they boulder or belaying them while they climb.

HOW IT ALL BEGAN

For as long as humans have been venturing into the mountains, some form of rock climbing has been a necessity. During the early 20th century, however, climbing began to take shape as a sport in its own right thanks to the passion of early pioneers in the UK, Germany and the United States. By the 1950s it was experiencing a surge in popularity. Specific climbing techniques were developed and specialist equipment to aid the safe ascent of a route was gradually introduced – often controversially – to the rock face.

Climbers at Yosemite National Park in California, USA, led the way during the 1960s and 70s pushing the limits of traditional (trad) climbing. Meanwhile sport climbing, in which climbers make use of bolts placed on a route, was developed in France during the 1980s and soon found a following with other European and American climbers. Since sport climbing reduced the amount of equipment that climbers needed to carry on a route, it allowed them to experiment with more gymnastic movements.

Sport climbing saw climbers attempting to control their environment outdoors. By the 1990s, this had been taken one step further with the construction of sophisticated indoor climbing walls. Nowadays, many people begin their climbing careers indoors.

Although the history of climbing is littered with men's names, women have played their part with records of female climbers making ascents in the Alps dating back to the late 1700s. At the beginning of the 21st century, women make up around 25 per cent of those participating in the sport and a handful have now carved out a name for themselves as modern climbing legends.

BODY AND MIND BENEFITS

Climbing is one of the most effective full-body workouts you can do. It improves muscle tone and definition, works the abdominals and strengthens the legs, back, shoulders and arms. If you're climbing outdoors, you often have to walk in to routes, which will also improve your cardiovascular fitness. You can start climbing at any age and you don't have to be super fit, just prepared to have a go.

As well as the physical benefits, climbing helps to develop many psychological skills, too. Route planning and problem solving on the rock promote mental agility, toughness and decision-making. What's more you have to have an acute awareness of risk and safety, and be 100 per cent focussed on the sport. Learning to take responsibility for you and your climbing partner helps you to build trust in yourself and others.

Girls who... Climb

Louise Alexander, 30-something,
Founder of Mountaingirl

'It's not just the mental and physical
side of climbing that I love. For me, it's
spiritual too. As well as taking you up
into the mountains where you are
surrounded by amazing scenery,
climbing forces you to grow up and
learn more about yourself than you had
ever realised. You have to be very
honest; climbing is an intense
experience during which friendships are
formed very quickly.'

GETTING STARTED

BOULDERING
The most pared-down form of climbing, bouldering is climbing on rocks – indoors or outdoors – that are only one or two metres from the ground. Although it can be done alone, it is usually done in pairs, each of whom takes it in turns to *spot* the other. *Spotting* is when you stand just behind and beneath the person who is climbing to guide their fall.

INDOOR CLIMBING
These days you can find indoor climbing walls everywhere from state-of-the-art gyms to public sports complexes to dedicated indoor climbing centres. Indoor climbing centres are ideal for those who want to get to grips with the basics before they make the transition to outdoors, and for those who live in the city and don't have easy access to outdoor routes. They're also great for winter training, when filthy weather conditions keep you off the rock.

Most indoor climbing centres run taster and introductory courses led by experienced climbing instructors. Such courses are essential for learning the rope and safety skills. They also provide the opportunity to meet other climbers and to build up a network of people with whom you can regularly climb. You can also hire all the equipment you'll need from the centre, which means you won't have to fork out a lot of money on gear while you're getting to grips with the sport.

SPORT CLIMBING
From indoor climbing walls most people find it easiest to begin their outdoor climbing careers on sport climbing routes. In *sport climbing*, climbers use the natural rock features to make their ascent. Similar to indoor walls, however, protection (along the route) and anchors (at the top) are permanently fixed on each route. This allows climbers to focus on movement and technique.

STAYING SAFE
With climbing, safety is paramount. Losing concentration for just one second could result in injury or, worse, death. The basic safety points to remember are:

- Look after yourself. Know your limits and ability. Check and double-check your equipment and ropes
- Look after others. Learn to belay correctly and watch out for your climbing partner at all times. Don't mislead others about the difficulty of a climb
- Tell someone where you're going and when you expect to be back
- Carry all necessary clothing, food and equipment you'll need
- Always take the safest route into a climb, and the safest route off a climb.

GRADES

Indoors and outdoors, climbing and bouldering routes are usually graded, with different grading systems for each. A route may be graded by the first person to climb it, but it may take many more climbs until a consensus is agreed on the final grade. However, there will be variations in the level of difficulty of routes of the same grade.

There are a number of systems in use. For instance, for bouldering you may see the Fontainebleau system, which is named after the famous bouldering area outside Paris. This ranges from 3 to 8c and sometimes carries the *Fb, Font* or *bloc* prefix. The US-equivalent V grades range from V0 to V15.

Meanwhile, at indoor walls, the climbing routes are most likely to be graded using French sports grades, which run from 3 to 9b+. For now, you should familiarise yourself with these grades as they will give you an idea of how technical a route is and provide an easy way for you to measure your progression.

When you start to climb outdoors, sport grades can help guide your choice of route, but they do not always account for the exposure of a route. It's therefore best to start off with a much easier grade than you are used to attempting indoors. Trad routes also have their own systems and, again, you should err on the side of easy when you first start out.

CLIMBING CLUBS

Joining a climbing club is a great way to meet other climbers with different levels of ability and experience, and to take part in organised trips to climbing routes, locally and further afield.

DIFFERENT TYPES OF ROCK

Sandstone Soft and crumbly, sandstone erodes easily to form lots of natural holds and features

Gritstone Harder and rougher than sandstone, gritstone nevertheless erodes in a similar way to sandstone, with plenty of natural holds and features

Igneous rock Found mostly in mountains, igneous rock is formed through centuries of volcanic activity. It offers a diverse range of natural features and is very hard

Limestone One of the most common types of rock in Europe, limestone is found both in the mountains and at sea level. Natural pockets in the rock act as handholds. Sport climbing is often done on limestone

Granite Granite rock formations provide some of the best places to climb in the world, including the Alps in Chamonix, France, and Yosemite National Park in California, USA. Depending on the type of weather and geological activity that it has been exposed to, granite takes on many different shapes and forms.

GEAR GUIDE

ROCK SHOES
Climbing or *rock shoes* usually have a soft suede or fabric upper and a grippy rubber sole. On really technical climbs, climbers wear a flexible shoe that provides them with as much 'feel' as possible on the rock. These shoes are very tight, which means that wearing them for more than an hour can be pretty uncomfortable.

At first, however, you'll need a shoe that is firm and flexible, not too soft and not too tight. Go for something that's half a size down from your normal street shoe – it's supposed to feel snug, but not agonising. This will support your feet while the muscles and tendons are still developing. Try on as many different shoes and brands as possible before you buy. Don't be swayed simply by what everyone else is wearing – your feet are unique.

Clean your rock shoes regularly with a nail brush and a little water. Dry the shoes off with a cloth and the rubber will be as good as new.

BEAUTY SPOT

Rock faces and rock shoes can play havoc with your nails. Keep your finger and toenails short and neat, and make sure you regularly indulge your hands and feet with a rich moisturising cream.

CLOTHING
Wear what's most comfortable and most appropriate for the environment. For indoor climbing, or on warm days outdoors, it's best to choose a *racer vest* teamed with tight-fitting *yoga* or *climbing pants* that allow you to move freely and are tailored enough at the bottom so that you can see your toes and feet.

Take a *fleece* to wear between climbs so that your muscles don't become too cool, and keep a pair of *flip-flops* handy to give your feet a break from rock shoes.

If you're climbing outdoors, be prepared for sudden changes in the weather, so always carry extra clothes in your backpack. This should include a pair of *water-resistant trousers, hat* and *gloves*, a *breathable wind- and water-resistant jacket* and a pair of *sturdy shoes* for the walk in. The colder the weather is likely to be, the more warmth and layers you should wear.

CHALK

Most climbing walls prohibit the use of *loose chalk* so initially you'll need to invest in a *chalk ball* and *bag*. When bouldering, don't clip the chalk bag onto your harness with a carabiner, as the hardwear may injure you if you fall. This is less of an issue on routes but, nevertheless, it's a good idea to wear your chalk bag on a belt or cord close to your body, which allows you to move it from side to side and easily access your chalk.

BOULDERING MATS

Like crash mats, *bouldering mats* are designed to cushion your fall. At indoor walls, bouldering mats cover the entire floor space surrounding the bouldering section. You can also get portable bouldering mats for use outdoors. As well as protecting the climber, they can help protect the vegetation and reduce erosion.

SAFETY STANDARDS

When buying equipment in Europe, check that it carries the CE (European Conformity) mark. This shows that it has met the safety standards set by the Union Internationale des Associations d'Alpinism (translated as the International Mountaineering and Climbing Federation; abbreviated to UIAA).

HARNESS

Unless you're bouldering, you'll need a safety *harness*. A well-fitting harness is essential. Try out a few in the shop before you buy one and, where possible, ask if the shop has facilities for you to hang in your harness. The harness should fit comfortably around your waist – not your hips – and you should feel happy hanging in it for at least 10 minutes. The leg loops should be secure, but not too tight.

Girls are best off getting a harness with adjustable drop back loops, so that you can go to the loo without having to remove the whole thing. There are now a number of the women-specific harnesses available.

Make sure you know how to wear and adjust your harness properly. Read the manufacturer's instructions and ask the shop assistant if you're at all unsure. Check your harness before every use for wear and tear, and retire it immediately if it has taken a major fall. It's not wise to buy a secondhand harness as you won't know the full history of its usage.

HELMET

On an introductory climbing course, you'll be expected to wear a *helmet*. Whether you decide to wear one at an indoor wall after you've completed the course, is up to you. Again, the decision is yours once you're outdoors, but in most cases you should consider it an essential piece of safety equipment. Your head is fragile and a helmet will protect your head from falling debris and most bangs against rock. Make sure the helmet doesn't wobble around on your head. If you're going to be climbing in cold conditions, get one that fits easily over a hat. Remember to take your beanie with you when you go to try on helmets.

BELAY DEVICES

A *belay device* works simply by putting a bend in the rope that creates friction and enables the belayer to hold the fall of the person who is climbing. There are a number of different belay devices available. To begin with, you'll need a *standard* (or *passive*) belay device that works well in most climbing situations and with a standard 10-millimetre rope.

CARABINERS

Carabiners (or *crabs*) are used to attach climbing equipment to your rope and harness. Most carabiners come in a 'D' or 'Offset D' shape. They are strongest when the gate on the carabiner is shut.

Snap-gate carabiners have either a solid or lighter wire gate that simply snaps shut. These are used for attaching the rope to *runners* on the climb and for attaching equipment to your harness. *Screwgate* or *locking* carabiners can be screwed shut and provide a secure method of attachment. *HMS* screwgate carabiners are generally used for belaying and tying into anchors.

ROPES

Climbing ropes are made of nylon and the most common type is a *kernmantel* rope. The rope's strength comes from an inner woven core, or kern, while an outer sheath, or mantel, protects the core from wear.

Ropes are usually provided at indoor walls and all you have to do is tie the rope into your belay and harness and start climbing with your partner. However, if your local wall does not provide ropes or you want to start lead-climbing indoors or climbing outdoors, then you'll need your own rope.

Ropes are classified as single or half and come in various lengths, weights and thicknesses to suit different climbing situations. To begin with, you'll need a single 10-millimetre mid-weight rope that's around 50 metres long.

ROPE TLC

Your rope is your lifeline. Look after it.
- Don't buy ropes secondhand
- Avoid borrowing other people's ropes or lending out your own
- Invest in a rope bag to protect your rope when you're carrying it and when you place it on the ground, indoors and outdoors
- The best way to store a rope is to coil it
- You can clean your rope by placing it inside a pillow case and putting it in the washing machine on a cold wash or simply by washing it in a cool bath. Use soap flakes or professional rope cleaner as these are softer than normal detergents
- Try to keep your rope out of strong sunlight and avoid placing it on the ground when you're in a car park, as the fumes from the tarmac can damage the rope
- Check your rope regularly for soft spots, which may be a sign of damage. To do this, roll the rope through your fingers, pinching it into

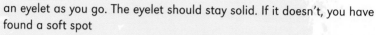

an eyelet as you go. The eyelet should stay solid. If it doesn't, you have
found a soft spot

- There are no rules for how long a rope should last. If you don't want any
doubts, then it's wise to retire your rope after around 150 days of use
- Immediately retire your rope after a major fall.

BACKPACK

A backpack is the most comfortable and convenient way to carry your climbing
equipment, clothing, food and water. You can get backpacks specifically
designed for climbing, which are slimmer than other backpacks and have loops
on the side for carrying equipment.

RACK

When sport climbing outdoors, you'll only be carrying a basic *rack* of equipment.
Along with your belay device and chalk bag this will include quickdraws, which
you clip to the gear loops on your harness. A *quickdraw* consists of two
carabiners linked by a 10- to 30-centimetre sling. These are used to create
runners between the protection and the rope, which helps to minimise the length
of a fall.

BASIC TECHNIQUES

BOULDERING

For beginners, bouldering allows you to practise balance and movement
techniques, build up your strength and train your muscles and tendons, and
begin to learn how to problem-solve, without having to go anywhere near a
harness or a rope.

From a safety perspective, it's best to go bouldering in pairs outdoors, so that
one person can spot while the other climbs. Initially, choose somewhere with a
flat landing and use a bouldering mat to reduce the impact of a fall.

Before you begin climbing, study the boulder and try and work out a *problem*. This could be a series of anywhere between two or 20 moves that you are going to traverse at the same height from one part of the boulder to the next. As you move through the problem, you can ask you partner to help you identify the holds.

TYING-IN
Aside from bouldering, most other forms of climbing use a rope safety system in which the rope should be securely tied to your harness.

Find the tie-in point for your harness. Now, tie a *figure of eight* knot about one metre from the end of the rope, thread the shortest length of the rope through the tie-in loop on your harness and then rethread it through the figure of eight. This is known as a *rethreaded figure of eight*. Secure it with a stopper knot. Make sure both knots are tight and compact, and sit close together.

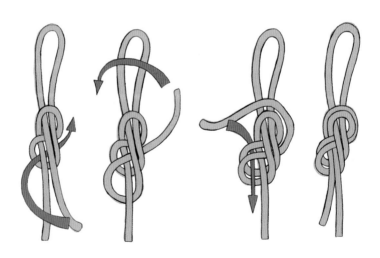

RETHREADED FIGURE OF EIGHT

BELAYING

At one end of the rope is the climber tied-in to their harness; at the other is the belayer, responsible for holding the climber's fall with the rope.

To create a belay, thread the end of the rope through the top of your belay device and then create a small loop the same size as the belay cord or wire before you rethread it into the bottom of the device. Secure the belay device to your harness with a rounded or HMS-style screwgate carabiner. The carabiner should go through the loop in the rope, as well as the cord or wire on the belay device that stops it from sliding down the rope. Double-check that the carabiner is screwed tight.

To belay, take up the slack on the rope and stand just in line with the climber. Keep one hand on the rope at all times. As your partner begins to climb, feed the live rope through the belay device and pull down and back on the dead rope to lock it off. Keep the dead rope taut, letting it out slowly and smoothly as the climber makes their ascent.

TOP-ROPING

The simplest way of tackling a route is to climb it with an anchor (or anchors) already secured at the top of the route. In this situation the rope is threaded through a top anchor, with the belayer on one end of the rope and the climber tied into their harness on the other.

When you start climbing indoors, you'll almost always use a top-rope and belay from the bottom of the route. In this set-up, when the climber has reached the top of the route they can simply be lowered back down to the ground on the rope. Outdoors, you may be belaying from the top or the bottom of the route.

LEAD CLIMBING

Once you've got used to top-roping you may want to move onto the next challenge – lead climbing. It's an entirely different experience from top-roping as the fear of falling can really start to kick in. To be successful, you've got to be sure that you're balanced at every stage of the climb and confident that your belayer knows how to belay, and to stop a leader fall softly.

In lead climbing the rope is not anchored to a top point. Instead, the *leader* secures the rope as they climb. At an indoor wall, there's usually a set of runners already placed along a route. The leader climbs the route, clipping the rope into the runners as they go. You can either clip the rope in when the runner is just above you, or when you are parallel to the runner. If you fall, you'll fall twice the distance of the rope from the last runner. So, to minimise the impact of your fall, you need to place runners at regular intervals on the climb.

Once the leader has reached the top of the route, they clip the rope into the top anchor before being lowered to the ground by the belayer. The leader now takes over as belayer and the *seconder* climbs the route, unclipping the rope on the way up. At the top, the seconder is lowered to the bottom and the rope is then simply pulled out of the top anchor and falls to the ground.

The principle is the same for sport climbing – the leader either threads the rope through fixed bolts or through a carabiner or quickdraw clipped into the bolt. At the top there are usually one or two fixed anchor bolts.

CLIMBING CALLS

When you're climbing, you need to keep communication clear with your partner. Limit what you say to one or two words, as your partner may not hear a whole sentence. You can use these common climbing calls:

Climbing! 'OK, I'm climbing now so pay attention and belay me'

On belay! 'OK, I've got you on belay and am watching you'

Watch me! 'I'm not sure about this move and might fall,' or 'I am likely to fall,' or 'I'm going to take a whipper right now so catch me!'

Slack! 'Give me slack/more rope'

Take! or *Tight!* 'Take in the slack of the rope'

Safe! 'I'm at the belay/anchor point.' Sometimes this can mean 'Take me off belay,' so it's crucial to discuss this with your belayer before you climb

Off belay! 'I'm not belaying you anymore'

That's me! After the rope is pulled in on a multi-pitch, the seconder says this so that the leader/top belayer knows that there's no more rope to pull in and to start belaying them up

Climb when ready! or *Climb on!* What the top belayer/leader says to the seconder, meaning 'It's OK to climb now, I have you on a belay'.

WARMING UP

Before you start climbing, it's essential to warm up. This reduces the risk of injury and will make your session easier and more enjoyable. A brisk walk or cycle ride to your local indoor wall will get your blood circulating, as will a walk into an outdoor route. Once you're kitted up and ready to go, spend a few minutes loosening up all the joints in your body, bending your elbows, circling your wrists, rotating your hips and shoulders, circling your feet and ankles, and so on. Follow this by stretching the major muscle groups and then begin your session with a few easy climbs. Bouldering is an ideal warm-up activity.

BALANCE AND MOVEMENT

If you're worried about your upper body strength, or lack of it, don't be. The most efficient climbers climb with their legs. Learn to trust your feet, keep your weight on your skeleton and always try to be in a position of balance. Rather than simply taking instruction from others, make your own decisions about moves from the outset. Plan your first few moves before you start, and keep on planning as you go.

Don't be afraid to twist and turn your body and look around for foot- and handholds; climbing a rock is not like climbing a ladder. Keep your body working in opposition – for instance, place your left hand in a hold and then move your right foot up – and aim for a series of smaller moves rather than making big reaches with your hands or taking high steps with your feet.

FOOTWORK
Good footwork is key to climbing. Don't place the entire body of your foot on a foothold, as this provides little room for manoeuvre. Instead, place the tips of your toes on the foothold so that you can swivel in different directions. Rock shoes have very grippy soles, so make use of them by *smearing* the sole of your foot to grip onto a smooth slab of rock. If there aren't any obvious footholds, try *edging* – balancing on the inside or outside edge of your foot. Another technique is to *jam* your foot into cracks.

HANDHOLDS
The easiest handholds are *jugs*, big holds that allow you to take a firm hold of the rock. An upside down jug is called an *undercut*. Smaller than jugs, *incut fingerholds* allow you to curl your middle finger joints over the hold. *Fingerholds* are even smaller and will only accommodate the tips of your fingers. Meanwhile you can use *sideways holds* of different sizes to keep your balance or to pull you across the rock.

Palming is a bit like smearing – you place your hand flat against the rock for grip and push down on it to give you purchase on the rock while you move your foot. The opposite of palming is *jamming*, when you jam your hand, fist or fingers into a crack. When using a handhold, keep your arms straight as this uses less energy and is more comfortable than bent arms.

WHOLE BODY MOVES
To climb a large crack, or chimney, you can press your feet on one side of the crack and your back on the other, slowly edging up the crack by moving your hands and your feet. This is called *chimneying*.

Bridging is when you straddle two sections of a rock to achieve a secure, stable position. This can be a good resting position. More strenuous is *laybacking*, where you pull back on a crack or vertical edge with your hands and push away with your feet.

When faced with an *overhang*, first balance your feet and then find an undercut to hold onto with one hand. Reach over the lip with your other hand to find a good handhold. Once you're happy with this, lift your feet off their holds and pull yourself up and over the overhang. Neither of these moves are easy, though, so you'll need lots of practice.

Finally, *mantelshelfing* (or *mantling*) is essentially climbing onto a flat ledge. Approach the ledge by looking for footholds that will get your feet as far up as possible. Then, push down on your feet until you can place your palms flat on the ledge. Push down on your palms and, once your arms are straight, bring one leg up to the side and put your foot on the ledge. Now, straighten your leg and, still using the strength in your arms, bring your whole body up onto the ledge.

FALLING
It's inevitable – at some point you're going to fall. So, relax, and get used to the idea. When climbing, keep the rope in front of you at all times to limit the risk of it wrapping around a leg if you fall. If you know you're about to fall, then push back off the wall with your hands and feet. Hold the knot above the rope on your harness to help keep you upright – *never* grab onto rope that's running through the runners. Stick your feet out to protect you in case you swing back onto the rock.

MENTAL ATTITUDE
While a little bit of anxiety is good for your climbing to focus your mind and keep you alert, over-anxiety can stop you in your tracks. To combat fear and panic, be clear in your head about the *perceived risk* ('I'm 10 metres above the ground and I'm going to die if I fall') and the *actual risk* ('I'm 10 metres above the ground, but my harness is attached to a safety rope that is anchored at the top of the route and I am confident that my belayer can hold me if I fall'). Relax, take deep breaths, and refocus on the situation. Have confidence and belief in your ability and try some positive thinking or self-talking – 'I am safe', 'I can do this', 'Keep going'.

Girls who... Climb

Lucy Darkin, 34, Project Manager

'Climbing takes considerable mental stamina. I get out of my comfort zone pretty frequently and, because I'm committed to a rock face, I have to dig deep and even say to myself out loud that I can do it, or enter into a bit of self-motivational chat – or, occasionally, considerable swearing! Once I nearly cried two-thirds of the way up a 10-pitch route. Climbing has certainly given me mental strength in other areas of my life too, such as coping with stressful situations.'

TAKING IT FURTHER

You'll find endless bouldering problems to attempt indoors and outdoors. Meanwhile, once you're confident with top-roping and leading climbs indoors and on sport climbs, why not move onto *trad* (see p50)? Once you've done a number of single-pitch climbs, try some *multi-pitch climbs*. Before you do so, however, you'll have to learn how to place your own *anchors*, *build belays* between pitches, and learn new knots and more advanced rope skills, including *abseiling* and setting up a *double-rope*. And, as your climbing career develops, you may find yourself travelling the world with ambitions of going *Alpine climbing* amid stunning mountain scenery, *ice climbing* in Scotland with the aid of picks and crampons, or attempting multi-day *big wall climbs* in California.

TRAD CLIMBING

Traditional or *trad climbing* is often regarded as the most pure form of climbing as climbers must place their own temporary *protection* (metal gear such as *cams* and *nuts*) along the route. The lead climber places the protection, the seconder removes it. The transition from indoor and sport climbing to outdoor trad climbing can present a steep learning curve. But, if you're keen, get together with an experienced instructor or friend and go for it.

CLIMBING FIT

CLIMBING
Climbing requires the use of specific muscles and tendons that are hard to develop off the rock, so climbing really is the best way to get fit for climbing. Happily, indoor climbing centres should make this relatively easy.

Try these three easy climbing drills:
- At the bouldering wall, work out a five- to eight-move problem that uses a variety of holds and angles. Begin by tackling the problem using mainly big holds that are quite far apart. This will build your arm strength. Then, tackle the problem by using smaller holds to develop your finger and forearm strength.
- Tackle a pyramid of four boulder problems or climbing routes of over 25 moves long. Start with easy routes and gradually build up to harder ones, then work back down the pyramid again. Aim to complete each route in under 10 minutes, rest for five minutes between each route.
- Choose a long problem or route of over 25 moves. Climb the route in under 15 minutes, stopping to 'hover' for 5-10 seconds between each move. Rest for five minutes between each attempt. Repeat one to three times.

When you first start training, it's important not to overdo it as your muscles will develop much quicker than your tendons. Limit sessions to two or three times a week and make sure that you're fully rested in between.

CROSS-TRAINING
A good level of general aerobic fitness will benefit your climbing. Aim to swim, run or bike at a moderate intensity for a minimum of 30 minutes at least twice a week. Walking and hiking are also great for boosting your fitness and will prepare you for those outdoor climbs where there may be a long walk into the route. Meanwhile, activities such as dancing and martial arts that raise your heart rate and improve muscle control and co-ordination will also complement your climbing.

FLEXIBILITY
Regular stretching is crucial for flexibility, which can reduce the risk of injury, reduce muscle tension and make movement easier and less tiring. After you've been climbing, stretch out all the muscles in your legs, back and upper body, and include forearm and wrist stretches, and ankle rotations. You may also want to join a regular yoga class – people who practise yoga are often very good at climbing.

ROCK FUEL

To survive a day out on the rock, make sure you have a healthy breakfast based on wholegrain carbohydrates, along with a portion of protein. Try smoked salmon and scrambled eggs on a wholegrain bagel or muesli with chopped banana, semi-skimmed milk and yoghurt. On a long climb, you probably won't have time to eat a lunchbox lunch. So, instead, eat little and often, grazing on snacks such as dried fruit and nuts, oatcakes and healthy muesli bars. Remember to keep well-hydrated too. It's tempting not to drink too much water so you don't have to go to the loo, but it's really important to keep your fluids topped up as even the slightest dehydration can dramatically affect your performance.

Girls who... Climb
Faye Page, 32, Environmental Consultant

'Climbing is a wonderful sport that's brilliant for women. When I started I rarely saw two girls climbing together at the crag, but now there are loads of girls doing it. You can be at any level and either work at it to improve, or just have fun at the level you're at. It makes you stronger and fitter, you get to see some amazing places and, for me, it's been a real confidence booster in other areas of my life.'

CLIMBING TRAVEL

DECIDING WHEN AND WHERE TO GO

You can easily find out about local climbing centres through your council or tourist office, or through organisations such as the British Mountaineering Council (BMC). Initially it's safest to climb outdoors with an instructor or with more experienced climbers who know where to go. At some point, however, you'll want to try new routes for yourself. In which case, you can make use of the plethora of climbing guidebooks available, which provide maps of named and graded routes. Climbing magazines are also a good source of routes. You can climb at any time of year, and you can stay close to home or travel abroad. But, wherever and whenever you go, always check the local weather forecast and dress appropriately for the conditions.

PACKING YOUR KIT

The great thing about climbing is that the gear is fairly minimal – well, unless you start trad or ice climbing – so you don't have to worry about weight restrictions on airlines or adding racks to your car.

When packing your kit, make sure your ropes are well-protected and won't come into contact with any sharp objects. If you're travelling by plane, put your shoes and harness in your carry on luggage just in case your flight is delayed. You don't want to miss a day's climbing at the beginning of your holiday.

TOP FIVE PLACES TO CLIMB...

...in Europe
Peak District, UK
Sardinia, Italy
Costa Daurada, Catalonia, Spain
Kalimnos, Greece
Chamonix, France

...worldwide
Trango Towers, Pakistan
Yosemite, California, USA
Smith Rock, Orgeon, USA
Western Cape, South Africa
Karnataka, India

FIND OUT MORE
www.theuiaa.org International Mountaineering and Climbing Federation

IF YOU LIKE CLIMBING, TRY...
Canyoning
Coasteering
Caving

JARGON BUSTER
Big wall climbing Born in Yosemite Valley, California, big wall climbing is the practice of climbing a wall that takes more than one day to complete. Climbers must haul their equipment with them and camp out on flat or artificial ledges

Bouldering Climbing on big boulders. No need for ropes or harness as you don't climb more than a metre or safe falling distance from the ground

Deep water soloing Climbing a route above water without the use of any protection or a rope. The climber relies on the water beneath them to protect them if they fall

Flashing Climbing a route or a boulder problem with some prior knowledge of the climb, but without any falls

Free climbing Climbing a route without using gear to have a 'rest'. The route may be protected with gear and a rope, but the climber relies solely on their balance and ability to make their way up the route. Not to be confused with soloing

Multi-pitch A lead climb which takes two or more stages for both climbers to reach the top of the route

Onsighting Climbing a route or a boulder problem without any prior knowledge of the climb, and without any falls

Single-pitch A lead climb in which both climbers reach the top of the route on the first ascent

Soloing Climbing a route without the use of any protection or a rope

Whipper A big fall.

03

THE GIRL'S GUIDE TO
MOUNTAIN BIKING

WHAT IS IT?

Mountain biking is going off-road on a bike designed to handle every kind of surface on the ground, from gravel to mud to rocks and roots. On a road bike you are restricted to the tarmac and must battle with other road traffic. But, on a mountain bike (MTB) a whole new world opens for you to explore. You can trundle along a country lane, before veering off-road along bridleways, firetracks and winding single track, following whatever route takes your fancy. Or, you can head to a trail centre, where marked trails specifically constructed for mountain bikers take you up and over mountains, through forests and across moors, with all manner of gruelling ascents, wild descents, and tricky jumps and obstacles to negotiate along the way.

BODY AND MIND BENEFITS

Not only does it work your legs giving you toned calves, thighs and bum muscles, mountain biking on uneven terrain also helps strengthen your core, back and upper body. As it's a non-load bearing form of exercise, unlike other activities such as running, your frame is supported while you work out, reducing the risk of injury. The sport will also give your cardiovascular fitness an intense boost and, depending on how hard you push yourself, you can burn a whopping 300 to 600 calories per hour. Every minute of your ride will give you a sense of satisfaction and achievement as you conquer yet another root, rock, or scary bit of downhill. The concentration it requires forces you to focus on the moment and forget about your worries – and sharing such experiences with others can foster amazing friendships on the trail.

HOW IT ALL BEGAN

Ever since it was invented, the bicycle has been ridden off-road. But, the birth of bikes designed specifically for the challenges of multi-terrain is hard to pinpoint. It could have been as early as 1896, when US infantry, the Buffalo Soldiers, rode from Missoula, Montana, to Yellowstone, California, to test their customised military bicycles in cross country conditions. Or it could have been thanks to the group of 20 French cyclists who made up the Velo Cross Club Parisien (VCCP) and took their souped up 650-B bikes on and off-road during the 1950s.

Nevertheless, most people believe that the modern day sport put its strongest roots down in 1970s Marin County, USA, where mountain biking naturally evolved out of Californians' love of hiking and adventure. Quite simply, you could cover a lot more ground in a day on a bike than you could on your feet.

Marin County is still a mecca for mountain bikers, but the sport has also rapidly spread around the world, with prime biking territory to be found as far and wide as Wales and Chile. At the same time, MTBs have become increasingly sophisticated and, while *cross-country* (XC) mountain biking is still the most popular, there are now subdivisions of the sport, including *downhilling* (DH), *freeriding* and *dirtjumping*.

Typically, women have first been coaxed onto the trails by their boyfriends. However, these days they don't need so much encouragement and many are realising that hitting the trails is just as much fun for the girls as it is for the guys.

GETTING STARTED

FIND YOUR WHEELS
If you already own a passable MTB that you use around town, great. If not,

borrow or hire one. Then, find some easy off-road riding nearby – trails through your local woods, say – and get a feel for what it's like to cruise across tougher terrain. By this time, you'll probably start to get hooked on the idea of being able to explore the countryside under your own steam and may have experienced the rush of whizzing down the odd gravel firetrack. This is when you should start thinking of investing in your first proper MTB.

Girls who... Mountain Bike

Sarah Burdon, 29, Co-founder of Flowmtb

'With mountain biking I love that I can go out one day and totally challenge myself and really push what I'm able to do, and the next day go for an easy ride but still have loads of fun. It's an amazing feeling after a ride when you're tired, dirty but so happy – post-ride beers and cakes are great, too.'

YOUR FIRST BIKE

As you'll discover, there is a galaxy of MTBs to choose from. But, if this is your first bike and you want to cover some ground, and experience the satisfaction of climbing up steep trails as well as the excitement of adrenalin-fuelled descents, then your best bet is a *hardtail* designed for cross country (XC). This type of MTB is suitable for commuting or road training in the week, especially if you run it with semi-slick or slick tyres. You'll also get more for your money than a *full-suss* (full-suspension) MTB and it's a safer option if you want to buy secondhand.

The next thing to think about is *budget*. As far as MTBs are concerned, the sky's the limit and it's easy to get carried away. As a rule, though, you should spend as much as you can afford, since you'll generally get what you pay for. However, you certainly don't have to buy at the top end straight away.

Perhaps the most sensible approach is to buy a really good frame with a lower *spec* (specification) – that's the brakes, suspension forks, gearsets; all the little bits that make up a complete bike. Most manufacturers have different versions of the same frame on which all that differs is the colour and the spec. These parts can be gradually replaced so that you can eventually make up your dream bike.

Talk to other people about their MTBs, why they bought them and what they do and don't like about them. Have a flick through MTB magazines, which are always bursting with reviews of the latest models, and get an idea of what you can afford. Then, go down to your *LBS* (local bike shop) and try out as many bikes as you can – you'll be surprised how different two apparently similar bikes can feel. If you can, 'demo' a few bikes on the trails, too.

Women-specific bikes are available. Smaller women find these work best as they're designed to fit more petite bodies. However, most taller women say that the women-specific design makes no difference to their ride. Whatever you decide, make sure the bike fits. A good LBS should be able to advise you on the fit and feel and help you find the right frame size. Don't ever buy a bike that's too big just because it's a bargain.

BIKE SETUP

Establishing a correct *bike set up* is a must. This is a balance between finding the riding position that is most comfortable (so you stay in the saddle longer) and the position that is most efficient for pedalling (so you don't waste valuable energy).

You may not find the best set up immediately. Make little tweaks each time you are out on the trails and note how it affects your ride. Ask someone to help keep your bike stable while you make the adjustments:

1   To find the correct *saddle height*, sit on your bike with one pedal in the bottom position. There should be a slight bend in your knee when you place your heel on the pedal.

2   To find the correct *saddle fore/aft position*, sit on your bike with your hands on the handlebars and one pedal in the 3 o'clock position. Your elbow should be roughly in line with, or just behind, your knee when it is on the pedal.

HITTING THE TRAILS

Ideally, you want somewhere that offers a variety of terrain and gradients. You could start by doing short one- or two-hour rides in your area. Plan routes on a map, paying attention to access rights – for instance, in some parts of Europe it's fine to ride on footpaths, in others it's not. Firetracks and bridleways usually offer good choices.

Then you can start planning trips further afield and explore parts of the country that you might not otherwise visit. Look through MTB guidebooks for ideas. These usually describe a number of tried-and-tested routes of different lengths and to suit a variety of abilities. If you arrive in an area unprepared, then find the nearest LBS and ask them about the best places to ride.

Alternatively, find out about dedicated MTB trails and trail centres. The tourist office of the region you're intending to visit is a good starting point. Trail centres often have a number of well-signed, colour-coded, graded routes that range from relatively easy to extremely technical. With only minimum navigation needed, you can focus solely on your riding skills.

MTB CODE OF CONDUCT

- **Preparation** Plan for the unexpected, carry everything you'll need for the ride, and tell someone where you're going and when you'll be back
- **Control your bike** Be aware of what's going on at all times
- **Know your ability** Only take on descents or obstacles that match your skills and experience. Dismount if you need to. When you plan a route, make sure that it is achievable for your level of fitness
- **If you get lost, retrace your steps** Don't run the risk of getting even more lost
- **Consider other countryside users** Respect rights of way, share the paths and trails with other users and always give way to walkers and horse riders. Let other trail users know you're coming with a friendly call or a bell
- **Leave without a trace** Take litter home. Stick to established trails so that you don't cause unnecessary erosion to the countryside
- **Close gates behind you** And leave property as you found it
- **Never scare animals.**

MTB CLUBS

Mountain biking can be a very sociable sport and MTB clubs usually welcome riders of all levels. Typical club calendars include a regular weekday ride, with longer rides at weekends. You'll be riding with a range of different abilities, which will help you develop your fitness, skills and confidence, and you'll never be stuck for someone to ride with, even in winter.

MTB FUEL

Whether you're heading out for a two-hour or day-long ride, it's important to keep your energy and hydration levels topped up. Don't underestimate the amount you need to eat and drink on the bike.

A small daypack with a rear pocket to accommodate a water bladder with a drinking tube and valve is the most convenient way to keep hydrated, as it allows you to take regular sips without having to stop mid-ride. You can also attach a cage to your bike to carry an extra sports bottle. Fill this with juice or an energy drink for when you need a liquid hit of calories.

MTB MAINTENANCE

As a beginner, all you need to know is enough to get you home should there be a problem on the trail – that is, how to change an inner tube (see below), how to change your brake pads, and how to fix a chain. Later on you might want to learn how to fix a puncture, index gears and tighten gear cables, and tighten a loose headset.

Anything that can only be fixed in the workshop can be learnt after the essentials – or taken to your LBS. Some things, such as servicing suspension forks, should be left to the experts. Hands-on is the best way to learn bike maintenance skills and many LBS now run short courses.

HOW TO CHANGE AN INNER TUBE

If you get a flat on the trails, the easiest thing to do is change your inner tube.

You'll need:
- spare inner tube (make sure the valve on the tube matches the one on your bike)
- tyre levers
- set of Allen keys (if you don't have quick release wheels).

What to do:
1. Remove the wheel. This should be easy if you have quick release wheels, otherwise use an Allen key.
2. Deflate your tyre by letting the air out of the valve.
3. Insert a tyre lever between the tyre and the rim near the valve. Hold the lever in place, or hook it to a spoke.
4. Insert a second tyre lever a few centimetres away from the first and run it around the rim to remove the tyre.
5. Remove the punctured tube.
6. Check the tyre for any objects that may puncture the new tube.
7. Push the valve of the new tube through the rim and inflate enough to give a little shape.
8. Insert the tube all the way around the inside of the tyre.
9. Push the tyre back onto the rim, working from opposite sides of the rim. Check that the tube has not got caught outside or pinched in the rim.
10. Inflate your tyre to around 35 to 45psi. Go ride!

CLEANING AND SERVICING YOUR BIKE
Every time you come back from a muddy ride – or every few rides if you're riding in dry summer conditions – clean your MTB. Look after your bike properly and it

will look after you on the trails, last much longer and will cost you less in the workshop.

Avoid the temptation to use a high-powered jet wash at the trail centre or garage. Instead, fill a bucket with warm water and add a small amount of light detergent. Wash down the frame with a sponge. Carefully clean the brakes, chain and gearset with an old toothbrush, removing all trace of grit and debris such as leaves and small sticks. Dry the bike with a soft cloth. Lightly lubricate the chain and gears by running drops of oil along the chain and then turning the chain through the cogs. Finally, clean the gear cables by loosening them off and running a cloth along the inner cables.

You should also get your mountain bike serviced regularly. At the beginning and end of the autumn/winter season is the minimum.

GEAR GUIDE

MTB GEOMETRY

There are two basic types of mountain bikes: hard tail and full-suspension (*full-suss*). In between, over and above, there are never-ending variations of the two with more or less *travel*, and different *geometry* to favour different terrains and different styles of riding. There are four main things to remember about geometry:

Head angle The head angle typically ranges between 65 and 75 degrees, where 65 is slack and 70 is steep. The higher the angle number, the steeper the head angle. A steep head angle is easier to handle on technical climbs, but feels less stable on descents; a slack head angle is easier to control at speed, but is less responsive on slower, technical sections. A head angle of 67 degrees is ideal for a bike with five inches of travel.

Bottom-bracket height The higher the bottom-bracket the more clearance you will have over rough terrain; the lower the bottom-bracket the lower your centre of gravity and the more control you will have on tight corners and turns. Bottom

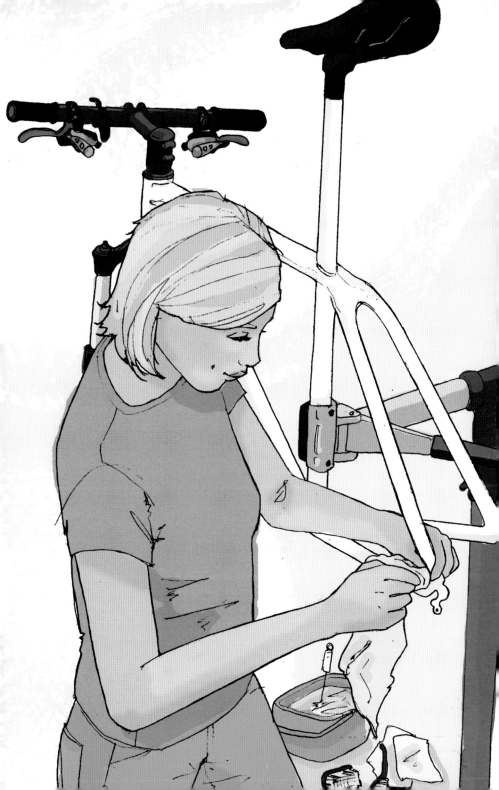

bracket height is measured in inches and typically ranges between 12 and 14 inches, where 12 is low and 14 is high. A bottom bracket height of 13.5 to 14 inches is the ideal height for a full-suss MTB.

Chainstay length A short chainstay gives you greater traction for climbing and more control for cornering. Ideally, look for a chainstay length of between 15.5 and 17.5 inches.

Seat angle A steep seat angle gives you optimal pedalling power and is better for climbing; a slacker seat angle gives you more control on the downhill.

MTB ANATOMY

Saddle When you're buying an MTB, don't worry about the saddle it comes with. Saddle fit is a matter of personal preference and they are inexpensive to upgrade. Women's saddles tend to be wider than men's to support the hips and pelvis, but try a range of saddles before you settle on one. When riding, tilt your saddle slightly forwards to help you on the ascents. Stay off the saddle for the descents and on technical sections of the trail.

Brakes Traditional cantilever or v-brakes that are still used on road bikes are now rarely seen on MTBs and have been superseded by disc brakes, similar to those used on motor bikes. Disc brakes stop the wheel in its centre, as opposed to the rim, and are much more responsive and durable than v-brakes. Hydraulic disc brakes are preferable to cable disc brakes but, if you can't afford a hydraulic system initially, then upgrade later.

New disc brakes can be very sharp so will take some getting used to. Learn to recognise when the brake pads need changing (have a look, you'll be able to see they're worn down) and when you need to clean the brake cables or top up the brake fluid (your brakes will start to feel slack). You don't need to change the discs unless they get damaged.

Brake levers Tilt your brake levers so that they're in line with your forearm, wrist, hand and finger. Keep making small adjustments until you find the most comfortable position.

HARDTAIL MTB

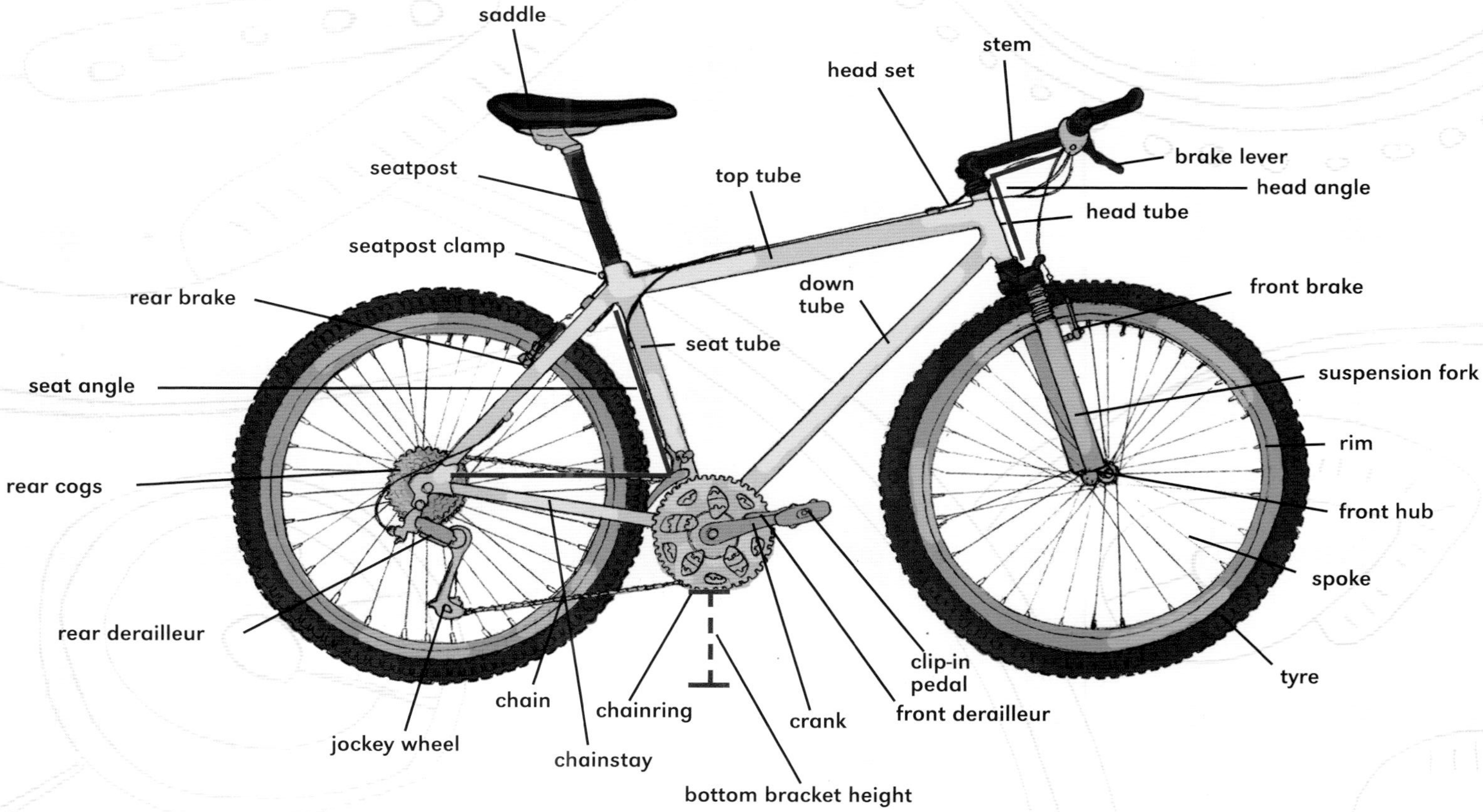

brake lever
head angle
suspension fork
front brake
rim
front hub
head tube
spoke
tyre
stem
head set
clip-in pedal
front derailleur
down tube
top tube
crank
bottom bracket height
seat tube
saddle
chainring
chainstay
chain
seatpost
seatpost clamp
jockey wheel
rear brake
seat angle
rear cogs
rear derailleur

Gears Most XC MTBs come with 27 gears. If your gears click or slip, they may need tuning or the gear cables cleaning or replacing. This is most common in winter when the cables are easily clogged with mud. Cleaning and replacing gear cables is a simple job and it will save you money in the long run if you learn to do it yourself rather than take it to the bike shop; tuning gears is a bit trickier.

Chain Check your chain regularly for kinks and loose links, and replace it every so often – they're cheap and keeping it well-maintained will cost you less than running a dodgy chain that damages your cogs and derailleurs. Don't over-lubricate (*lube*) your chain. Use a lubricator suited to the riding conditions.

Chainstay Your chain will slap on your chainstay when you ride, causing marks on the frame. You can buy chainstay guards, but it's easy to make your own with a piece of old neoprene wetsuit and a few plastic zip ties.

Pedals There are two basic options here: *flat pedals* and *clipless* or *clip in* pedals, otherwise known as *SPDs* (Shimano Pedaling Dynamics; after the first clipless pedals) or *'spuds'*. Flat pedals are safest for learning as your feet are free to come off the pedals whenever you lose your balance. Worn with flat rubber-soled shoes, they're also better for performing stunts.

The advantage of SPDs, however, is that you clip your feet into cleats on the pedals. This gives you maximum pedalling efficiency as you are able to transfer power from your legs to the bike through an entire 360° cycle, rather than just on the down stroke. Take time to make friends with your SPDs. When you first get your pair, practise clipping in and out at home, and then take them out onto very easy trails – choose those with grassy or loose banks for softer landings.

Suspension forks and *shocks* Designed to lessen the impact of riding over uneven and obstacle-ridden off-road terrain, *suspension forks* and *shocks* (a coil spring or air shock) are standard for most MTBs. On an XC hardtail bike there's a suspension fork at the front of the bike, but not at the rear. Full-suss bikes have front suspension forks and rear suspension shocks. XC hardtail bikes typically have between three and four inches of travel at the front, while full-suss DH bikes typically have between six and eight inches of travel at the front, and between six and 10 inches at the rear.

Some bikes allow you to lock out the suspension, which is useful if you're going to be riding your MTB on the road or on hard-packed even trails. You may also be able to adjust the *preload* on your bike to soften or stiffen the suspension according to the terrain. A stiffer suspension is better for climbs; a softer suspension is better for descents and going over obstacles. Avoid making your suspension too soft and hitting the bottom of your travel limit (*bottoming out*), though.

Tyres Most MTBs have 26-inch wheels run with knobbly tyre treads, which give plenty of traction over rough and rocky terrain. For the worst kind of muddy and grassy terrain you can fit spiky tyres with widely spaced knobs. Nearer to the road bike end of the spectrum are semi-slick tyres with more closely spaced side knobs that are best-suited to hard-packed trails.

Make sure your tyres are inflated to 35 to 45psi, or within the range indicated on your tyres. Start with the highest tyre pressure and then gradually let a little air out at a time until you find the pressure that feels right – you're aiming for a balance between speed and traction.

Stem and handlebars You can adjust your *stem height* and *length* to suit your riding style and position. A shorter stem is twitchier than a longer stem, but is good for control and 'play biking'; a longer stem gives you a more stretched out riding position and is usually favoured by endurance riders. Handlebar width is a matter of personal preference. If you ride a lot of narrow trails, then you may want to shorten your handlebars.

PROTECTIVE GEAR
Helmet Whether you go for a lightweight, well-ventilated cycle helmet, full-face motor-bike style helmet or a retro flat-top tortoise shell MTB helmet, it's up to you. Just wear one.

Gloves Padded MTB gloves with reinforced palms can prevent blisters and protect your hands if (or when) you fall. Use fingerless gloves in warmer conditions.

Body armour Knee and shin *pads*, elbow pads, shoulder pads, and chest and back *plates* offer increased protection. Wear whatever gives you confidence. A *bib* with thigh, knee and shin protection is ideal for beginners. You can get women-specific body armour.

Eye protection If you don't like the idea of being poked by branches, or dirt and grit flying off the trails and into your face, wear a pair of *clear-lens sunglasses* (for general riding) or *goggles* (for DH or freeriding).

Lights In case you stay out until dusk, carry a good pair of front and tail lights to get you home safely. Don't forget to carry spare batteries, too.

If you fancy a bit of *nightriding* (frightening first time, but excellent fun and great for developing skills), then invest in a proper set of nightriding lights. You can often hire these at trail centres in the winter, so you might like to try before you buy. Nightriding lights (worn on the front of the bike only) have a much more powerful beam than ordinary bike lights and enable you to see one or two metres ahead on the trail.

CLOTHING

TOPS
The key to dressing for mountain biking is *layers*. You want to be warm when you get going, but able to strip off some layers once you've worked up a sweat. Meanwhile, weather can change rapidly, especially when you're at the top of a mountain, with chilly breezes and slashing rain coming in from nowhere.

Start with a *supportive sports bra* underneath a base layer vest or crew and a *short-* or *long-sleeve front-zip cycling jersey*. Over this, wear a *lightweight waterproof or breathable cycling jacket*. It should taper down at the back to cover your bum and hips when you lean forward on the bike. Check the sleeves don't ride up past your wrists when you grab the handlebars. Between seasons, you could wear a sleeveless *gilet* instead of a jacket. Pack a warm fleece to pull on when you stop during the ride (like, for lunch). Obviously, you'll only need a pared down version of this if you're riding in a hot climate.

BOTTOMS

Perhaps the scariest part of dressing for mountain biking is the dilemma of what to wear on your bottom half. *Shorts* are the norm, but these can put fear into women with even the most svelte legs. There is a wide range of options available from capri pants to baggy shorts, so try out a few in the shop until you find the most flattering fit. Even when it's cool, you'll want to ride in shorts. However, really cold, foul weather calls for *tights* underneath a pair of *breathable waterproof trousers*.

Whatever you wear, though, make sure it's *padded*. This will reduce the likelihood of bruising and saddle soreness the next day. Note: you don't wear underwear with padded shorts or tights, so invest in at least two or three pairs for your MTB wardrobe.

DAYPACK

To carry all your essential on-the-bike kit, including spare layers, tool kit and snacks, you'll need a small *backpack* – make sure it can accommodate a water bladder and tube for drinking on the go (for more on this, see p10).

TOOLS

For basic MTB maintenance, a few tools will come in handy. The absolute minimum you should carry while out riding is a *pump, spare inner tube, tyre levers* (you could use a couple of metal dessert spoons) and a set of *Allen keys*.

BEAUTY SPOT

When you take a fall or hit on the trails, rub arnica cream into bruises to help them heal more quickly. For a double dose once you're back home, relax in a hot bath with Neal's Yard Seaweed & Arnica foam bath, which will also provide welcome relief for fatigued muscles.

BASIC TECHNIQUES

CLIMBING

Fitness obviously helps, but you can't rely on muscle alone to get you up steep climbs. Sit on the nose of the saddle and keep your centre of gravity low, with your elbows bent and chest towards the stem. Once you've practised this, try pulling your bars down and back towards the rear axle of the bike. This will give you greater pedal power and traction. Don't go too low on the gears as you'll lose traction and your wheels will start spinning out.

DESCENDING

As you approach a descent, first consider your speed. You don't want to fly into a descent and then have to brake in a mad panic. But, equally, you don't want to go too slow, as this will make it harder to get over rocks and roots on the trail. Trust your bike, relax, and let it roll freely over any obstacles. If you need to brake, do so on the smooth sections. Stay off the saddle and hover just above or, if the gradient is really steep, just behind it. Keeping your weight over the back of the bike will give you more control.

CORNERING

Look ahead and judge how tight the corner is, and if there are any roots or rocks that will affect your turn. Brake gently as you enter the corner as wide as possible and then turn into the apex or midpoint, immediately shifting your gaze to look out of the turn and down the trail ahead. Exit the corner as wide as possible. During the turn, your outside pedal should be at the bottom, with most of your weight over the outside pedal and your body positioned slightly forwards towards the handlebars. Lean into the turn so that the treads on the sides of the tyres are able to grip into the corner.

BERMS

Don't be intimidated by banked corners, called *berms*. Use them to your advantage and have fun with them. You don't need to worry about where to enter a berm, just keep pedalling and follow the bank around the turn. Keep your fingers off the brakes and lean at the same angle as the berm. Berms are steeper at the top than they are at the bottom. If you've dropped your speed, ride towards the bottom of the berm and don't lean too much. If you're going fast and have maintained your speed, ride at the top of the berm and lean more dramatically.

SWITCHBACKS

One of the hardest trail features to master are *switchbacks*. These are very tight turns found on both steep climbs and descents. When approaching a switchback on a climb, enter as wide as possible and follow the outside line of the switchback, maintaining your momentum with a few hard cranks on the pedals. On a descent, slow right down and enter as wide as possible, turn at the apex and then exit as wide as possible.

DROPS

A *drop*, or *drop off*, is a point in the trail where you have to drop from one level to the next. It's like riding down a step. To begin with, even tiny drops can be intimidating. Start small and take on gradually bigger ones as you grow in confidence and experience. If a drop is simply too much for you, dismount and walk your bike down.

When approaching a drop, maintain your speed. It may seem scary, but you'll hardly notice it if you keep up momentum. Position your weight over the back of the bike, crouch low and keep your front wheel level with or slightly above your rear wheel until you're airbourne. For flat landings, your rear wheel should land first. For downhill landings, your front wheel should land first.

ROOTS, ROCKS AND MUD

The best way to approach obstacles such as roots and rocks is head on, at speed. Stay loose and relaxed, let your bike roll over them, and be ready to rebalance yourself if you slip.

GEAR SELECTION

Correct gear selection is crucial. Keep your eyes ahead on the trail and anticipate the gear you'll need to make a climb or get over an obstacle. Shift up or down to the correct gear before you're in the section and try to keep up your cadence – you don't want to be spinning the wheels too slow, or too fast. Practise until you find the right balance.

When you're changing gears, keep your chain level across the front and rear cogs. You don't want the chain on the smallest cog at the front and the biggest at the rear, or vice versa, as this will stretch your chain and damage your gears.

BRAKING

The brakes are there to help you control the bike. Learn to use your brakes only when you really need them – don't constantly cling onto them for dear life. Anticipate what's ahead and react accordingly. Cover your brake levers with your index finger (not your whole fist!), brake hard to slow down and then let the bike roll freely. Don't drag the brakes. Slamming on the brakes suddenly will send you shooting over the handlebars or cause your bike to jack-knife.

LINE CHOICE

Look as far ahead down the trail as you can, pick a line that you want to follow, be confident in your choice and stick to it. If you're always looking at the trail immediately in front of you, it's only going to be a matter of time before your face hits the dirt. By all means ride behind more experienced riders and follow their line, but learn to make decisions yourself.

FLOW

When all your skills start to come together, you're enjoying the challenge, but you're not terrified by the trail, your bike feels like a part of you and you find yourself gliding over obstacles and flying over the drops, that's when you're really beginning to feel what it's like to flow. Flow is the smooth, relaxed, seemingly effortless experience of riding where everything just seems to click.

TAKING IT FURTHER

Once you've got to grips with some of the basic techniques, then you can move onto developing more advanced skills such as *bunny hops, manuals,* or *wheelies,* which are all essentially different ways of lifting your bike to get over obstacles and jumps. With more confidence and experience you can take on more technical trails with bigger obstacles, jumps and drops. If you love learning new tricks and stunts, why not have a go at freeriding or dirtjumping at a bike park? Or if you can't get enough of the descents and want to up the ante, why not have a go at downhilling? Many trail centres have specific trails and sections set aside for both. As you learn more about mountain biking, then you'll also want to improve your MTB maintenance skills, so that eventually you're able to build and tune your bike so that it has the perfect fit and feel for your style of riding.

Girls who... Mountain Bike

Hannah Wilson, 25, Specialized Deputy Store Manager

'At a downhill race people will ask you how you did or what line you took or, simply, if you want to go for a cup of tea. It's really friendly. I've made some brilliant friends through downhill, both male and female, and now feel comfortable riding with anyone.'

MTB FIT

BIKING

Of course, mountain biking will get you fit for mountain biking. However, it may not be practical to get out on your bike regularly, especially if it's a car drive to your nearest trails. But, that doesn't mean you can't ride during the week. Here's how:

- Commute to work and ride around town
- Stick your bike on a turbo trainer at home and ride while you watch TV
- Do a workout on the stationary bikes in the gym
- Join a local spinning class.

Try to vary your training to include interval training (where you alternate hard efforts with shorter periods of recovery) and hill climbs.

CROSS-TRAINING

Any other exercise that builds your cardiovascular fitness will improve your endurance on the trails. Walking is great for maintaining your base fitness, running provides excellent high-intensity training, and swimming is an impact-free form of training that's also very relaxing and can aid recovery after a hard ride.

STRENGTH TRAINING

The shock of riding across rough terrain and over obstacles, along with drops, jumps and inevitable falls puts strain on your body. Mountain biking also causes muscular imbalances. For instance, biking alone develops strong quadriceps while hamstrings remain relatively weak, and greater stress is put on the lower back muscles than on the abdominals. Regular strength training can help your body cope with strain and even out imbalances. Upper body strength training can be especially beneficial for girls.

Try to do a simple strength training circuit at home two or three times a week for 30 minutes, which includes press ups, calf raises, squats, crunches, lower back extensions and tricep dips.

FLEXIBILITY

Stretching will benefit your mountain biking in many ways. For instance, it will improve your posture, reduce your risk of injury and reduce muscle soreness. Make sure you stretch your neck, shoulders, back, groin, calves, hamstrings and quadriceps after every ride. A weekly yoga class will also help improve your flexibility.

Girls who... Mountain Bike

Jayne Kerridge, 33, Psychiatrist

'I hated sport at school, where it was all team stuff and really popular-girl-cliquey. It put me off sport for years, along with undiagnosed asthma. It was an epiphany to find a sport that was actually enjoyable and which takes you out into the lovely hills. Now, thanks to mountain biking, I'm a billion times fitter.'

MTB TRAVEL

DECIDING WHEN AND WHERE TO GO

The brilliant thing about mountain biking is that you can go anywhere, anytime, whatever the weather. At times when most people wouldn't dream of stepping outside, you can be on the trails getting muddy and dirty and having all the fun in the world. You could travel across the world with your bike, but often you don't need to go very far to find some amazing trails.

TRAVELLING BY CAR

If your car's big enough you can remove the front and rear wheels, if necessary, and pack your bike in the boot. Put a plastic sheet down first to protect your car interior from dirt and grease, and pad your bike with blankets and towels, especially if you're transporting more than one bike. Alternatively, fit a bike rack to the roof or rear of your car. Be careful not to load bikes too close together otherwise they may rub and scratch the paintwork.

TRAVELLING BY PLANE

Check the airline's policy on carrying sports equipment before you book your ticket. Pack your bike in a bike bag (the ones with wheels are easier to manoeuvre) or pick up a cardboard box from your LBS (call ahead to ask them to put one by for you). Remove your handlebars (from the stem), wheels (let a little air out of the tyres), rear mechanism and pedals. Pack and pad everything very carefully, so that each part of the bike is well-protected and isn't going to be dented or damaged in transit. You can use a block of wood or buy special braces to prevent your suspension forks from being pushed inwards, and put a piece of cardboard in between your brake pads to stop them clamping together. Once you've padded out the individual bits of your bike, wrap the bike in more padding, pack out the cardboard box and secure everything tightly.

TOP FIVE PLACES TO MTB...

...in Europe
Portes du Soleil, Morzine, France
Scotland
Wales
Lake Garda, Italy
Sierra Nevada, Spain

...worldwide
British Columbia, Canada
Moab, Utah, USA
New Zealand
Costa Rica
South Africa

FIND OUT MORE
www.imba.com International Mountain Bicycling Association

IF YOU LIKE MOUNTAIN BIKING, TRY...
Adventure racing
Cyclocross
Mountain bike orienteering

JARGON BUSTER
Dirtjumping Doing jumps and getting airborne on your bike
Downhilling Going down very steep trails at speed on MTBs designed specifically for this kind of riding
Flow The feeling of being part of your bike and effortlessly gliding down the tracks
Freeriding Doing tricks and stunts over jumps and obstacles
Full-suss A full-suspension bike with suspension forks at the front and a suspension shock at the back
North Shore Narrow sections of wooden manmade trails elevated on stilts, with undulating gradients, drops and see-saws
Section A piece of the trail or an area of the trail centre
Singletrack A narrow piece of trail, only wide enough for one bike
Spuds Clipless pedal system
Travel The amount of suspension that your mountain bike has in its front suspension forks, and/or rear suspension shock.

04

THE GIRL'S GUIDE TO
SNOWBOARDING

WHAT IS IT?

The younger sister of skiing, in which the skier races down snow-covered slopes with a ski on each foot and a pole in each hand for stability, snowboarding is done hands-free on a single board that has its origins in skateboard and surfboard design.

Snowboarding is all about poise, balance and subtle movements and riders control their board by applying gentle pressure through their feet. At one extreme there is freeriding, which is fast and often done off-piste; at the other is freestyle, with aerial tricks performed on manmade obstacles in snowparks.

HOW IT ALL BEGAN

Although accounts of early attempts at snowboarding date back to the late 1920s, the modern sport has its roots in Snurfing. A melding of the words 'snow' and 'surf', the Snurfer was invented in 1965 by chemical engineer Sherman Poppen from Michigan, USA, when he tied two skis together to make a toy for his daughter, Wendy.

However, it's East Coast skateboarder and surfer Dimitrije Milovich and Yankee carpenter Jake Burton who are regarded as the early innovators of snowboard design. In the mid-1960s Milovich took to the snow on a cafeteria tray and then began to make snowboards based on surfboards and skis. In 1979 Burton won the right to ride on his own design at the annual Snurfer contest in Michigan. His snowboard featured the first binding and Burton's name has now become synonymous with world-class snowboard equipment.

By 1985 snowboarding had been recognised as an official sport. Initially, though, ski resorts did not welcome snowboarders and many had to sneak onto the runs at night. But, come the early 1990s, most had dedicated areas for snowboarders and snowparks had also begun to crop up across North America and Europe.

For years, snowboarding was a male sport. Now it's a different story. These days it's hard to miss the increasingly confident contingent of snowboarding chicks who are shredding up the slopes, wowing crowds in major competitions, and producing their own snowboarding flicks.

BODY AND MIND BENEFITS

Snowboarding works your legs and is great for strengthening your thighs and buttocks. But, since you'll spend a fair amount of time pushing yourself up to standing, it works your upper body too. You can also expect your balance and coordination to improve. As a beginner, you'll burn around 350 calories per hour, while more experienced snowboarders burn around 450 calories per hour. Each time you go out on the slopes you'll experience a sense of achievement on numerous different levels – grasping and then gradually perfecting the basic techniques, progressing onto harder slopes, making your turns that little bit smoother, learning how to read the terrain and attempting new tricks. This will boost your confidence and self-esteem on and off the snow.

GETTING STARTED

BACK TO SCHOOL
Before you even think about hitting the slopes, find a decent snowboard school – not a ski school that simply offers snowboarding as an aside. You may have a very enthusiastic mate who's keen to teach you but, unfortunately, this may set your snowboarding off on the wrong foot.

Girls who... Snowboard

Laura Linneman, 28, Children's
Occupational Therapist

*'I find snowboarding so energising. If
you're a bit down at work or in your life,
you know a week of snowboarding will
have a really positive effect. I think it's
like a meditation too, as you focus on
nothing but the moment.'*

FITNESS FIRST

Typically, snowboarding holidays last just one or two weeks and aren't cheap. So,
to ensure that you get the best return on your investment and have as much fun
as you can, it's wise to arrive at the resort with at least a little base fitness. (For
tips, see Snowboard Fit, on p109.) Go easy on yourself during the first few days
as your body will be working hard to adjust to the lower oxygen levels at altitude.

DAY ONE

In your first lesson, your instructor should introduce you to your equipment, check
you're wearing the right clothing, explain how a snowboard works and check that

your bindings are set up correctly. Once you've done this and warmed up you'll start with the basic techniques. Lesson over, ask your instructor where to practice, take at least an hour's break, fuel up with a light lunch and make sure you're home by 5pm for a hot shower and some worthwhile stretching – you'll feel less stiff and more energetic for it the next day.

BUYING VS. HIRING GEAR

Snowboards look cool – they're meant to. But don't be tempted into buying a board before you board the plane or train just because you love the graphics. And, don't borrow your friend's old board either, it might not be right for you.

Your best bet is to hire a snowboard and bindings at the resort – ask your snowboard school for recommendations of rental shops. There are two main reasons for this: firstly, you probably don't know enough about snowboards and snowboarding at this stage to know what you want; and, secondly, if you buy a beginner board you may progress much quicker than you expected and grow out of it quite quickly.

Whether you hire or buy a board, make sure you go to a shop with knowledgeable staff. Tell them as much as you can about your ability and the kind of riding you do, along with your height, weight (though, eek, they'll probably have sized you up already) and shoe size. Some shops and snowboard schools offer demo boards, so you can try before you buy. Also look out for demo days held by snowboard manufacturers at the resorts.

However, if you know that you're going to go snowboarding at least once or twice a year, what's really worth buying is boots. Buy a comfortable pair and, as long as you look after them, they'll last a long time.

STYLES OF RIDING

Beyond the basic techniques, there are two main styles of snowboarding: freeriding and freestyle. *Freeriding* is all about making the most of what the natural terrain and snow conditions have to offer. Freeriders like going off-piste and exploring the back-country. And they like speed. They aim to flow down the mountain, carving turns and jumping obstacles as they make their descent.

Freestyle is for the exhibitionists of snowboarding and makes for compelling competitions. It's heavily influenced by skateboarding and the aim is to be able to pull off spectacular jumps and tricks in snowboard parks and on natural mountain obstacles. As you progress, you may find you lean towards one or the other. However, most people have a go at both and, for this reason, versatile *all mountain boards* are still the most popular.

SNOWBOARDING TERRAIN

Piste Maintained trails at resorts are given different grades or markings depending on their level of difficulty and are the place to learn and improve technique. Hit the slopes early to get the best of the *corduroy* (freshly groomed runs). As the day progresses, the pistes get busier and conditions become increasingly *bumpy* due to moguls cut by skiers. At some resorts you'll also find *itineraries*. These are marked but ungroomed runs that will give you a feel for what it's like to go *off-piste*.

Pipes Derived from snowboarders' desire to mimic skating and surfing terrain, a *halfpipe* is a manmade snow-covered U-shaped jump dug out of the snow that looks like a big pipe cut in half lengthways. A quarterpipe is half a halfpipe jump, with a single steep side.

Snowpark This is home to manmade obstacles such as rails, boxes and kickers, and is fun for learning a new trick or nailing an old one. It is usually very social. Remember to check out the park rules before you ride.

Off-piste These are areas of snow within the bounds of the ski resorts that aren't maintained but are controlled by *pisteurs* (ski patrol). Going off-piste is often simply a matter of ducking beneath the ropes and snowboarding in the areas between the runs. When you get perfect conditions with bottomless *powder* (freshly fallen snow) you can't beat it. But, on the flipside, rapidly changing weather conditions can spell danger, so don't venture off-piste until you have built up the knowledge and experience to stay safe.

Back-country This is unpatrolled terrain, aka wilderness, outside the bounds of the resorts where you'll find fresh powder and untouched tracks. But you may have to hike out to find them, which adds to the adventure. Fitness and mountaineering experience will help. But don't go without a qualified mountain guide, as there's no back up if you run into trouble.

PISTE GRADINGS

At the resorts pistes are graded according to level of ability and steepness of the slopes. Below is a guide to piste gradings around the world. Take them with a pinch of salt – two similarly graded pistes at different resorts can vary greatly in gradient and difficulty.

Europe
Green: Beginner
Blue: Easy
Red: Intermediate
Black: Advanced

USA, Canada, Australia, New Zealand
Green circle: Beginner to Easy
Blue square: Intermediate
Single black diamond: Advanced
Double black diamond: Advanced, much steeper slopes than you would find in Europe.

GETTING AROUND THE RESORTS
Tourist offices and lift pass offices at resorts should be able to provide you with a map of the resort and the pistes. Among other things, a piste map should show pistes, piste gradings, restaurants, and information and first aid points. It will also show how the pistes are linked by cable cars and chair and drag lifts. To use these you'll need a lift pass. You can buy passes that are valid from as little as half a day to a whole season.

LIFT OFF

Initially, one of the greatest challenges in snowboarding can simply be negotiating the lifts. Watch how other people do it before you have a go.

Cable cars are the easiest. Take off your board and join the queue. Place your board on the outside rack of the cabin – or take it in with you if it's full – step into the cabin, take a seat and admire the view. When you arrive inside the next cable car station, wait for the door to open, step out of the cabin and pick up your board.

Chair lifts Release your back foot from the bindings and skate into position on the ramp. As the chair lift pulls up behind you reach out for it with one hand, sit down, pull the safety bar down over your head and place your front foot on the foot rest. If there's no foot rest, place your back foot underneath your board to support the weight. To get off, lift the bar, place your board flat on the ground, pointing in the direction you want to go. Let the lift push you forward and then straight run off the lift and down the ramp.

Drag lifts With your back foot free, place it on the board in front of the back binding. Point your board in the direction you want to go. Grab the pole and place it between your legs. Hold your stance and use your back hand for balance. Let the lift drag you up the slope. When you reach the top, release the pole from between your legs and straight run to safety. If you're having trouble, you can buy a *stomp pad*, which will make it easier for your boot to grip the board when you straight run.

SNOW AND WEATHER CONDITIONS
There's much more to snow than you might imagine. From a distance, the pistes may all look the same, glistening beneath their white blanket, but when you're out riding you'll encounter a variety of conditions.

Freshly fallen snow or *powder* is what snowboarders crave most. It has a smooth, dreamy surface that can inspire feelings of weightlessness. It will cushion your landing when you jump, or if you fall. But, as the powder melts it begins to turn to *slush* and, with more people riding it, soft *bumps* begin to form. Or, when the powder becomes compacted, it will turn to *crud* with harder and less forgiving bumps.

When the sun's rays melt the top layer of soft powder and there is a cold wind, the surface becomes covered with a frozen *crust*. A hard crust is icy and difficult to ride; a soft crust can be dangerous as it's easy to break through the surface.

The trickiest conditions to ride, however, are *ice* and *hardpack*. It's a good idea to make sure your edges are sharp when you ride in these conditions. Hardpack forms when the snow has melted and frozen a number of times.

SNOW FUEL

You'll need plenty of energy for a day on the mountain, so make sure you get your nutrition right.

- Start the day with an energy-giving breakfast such as a bowl of steaming porridge with a handful each of sultanas, almonds and chopped apple
- Drink lots of water throughout the day as it's easy to get dehydrated at altitude. Avoid tea and coffee
- At lunch, steer clear of the stodgy cheese-laden mountain dishes that will make you feel sleepy
- A light meal such as a tuna sandwich on wholemeal bread, a healthy cereal bar and a piece of fruit will perk you up for your afternoon ride
- Carry a bag of dried fruit and nuts in your backpack or an energy bar for when you hit that 3 o'clock slump
- Finish the day with a hot, hearty meal. You deserve it.

PISTE ETIQUETTE
Respect the rules of the piste...
- Don't endanger yourself or others. Ride on pistes and at speeds suited to the conditions and your ability
- Look uphill before setting off or joining a piste
- If you stop on a piste, make sure you can easily be seen
- When in a group, stick together; don't spread yourselves across the slope
- Overtake on the right or left, but leave plenty of clearance between you and other piste users
- Pay attention to signs and markings on the piste
- When descending or climbing on foot, keep to the sides
- If you see an accident, stop and help. Make sure other piste users can see there's been an accident and inform the ski patrol.

Meanwhile, a dense cloud cover can cause *flat light* which can reduce visibility on the mountain and make it difficult to see any undulations or the angle of the slope. This is called a *white out*.

The way a slope faces, known as its *aspect*, also affects the snow. As the temperature rises throughout the day, conditions on a south-facing slope, for instance, may change more noticeably than those on a north-facing slope that sees very little of the sun. Check the local forecast for wind direction, too, as you'll want to avoid wind-beaten slopes.

Before you consider going off-piste into an uncontrolled area, take proper precautions. The International Scale of Avalanche Hazard Rating ranges from one to five, with one being low risk and five being extreme. But, it's not quite that simple. Different slopes present different hazards and, unless you're skilled in understanding and testing the conditions, you're likely to put you and your colleagues in extreme danger. So, wise up and book yourself onto a reputable mountain and avalanche safety awareness course.

Girls who... Snowboard

Tammy Esten, 29, Founder of Mint
Snowboarding

'I love the sense of freedom that
snowboarding gives me and I love
being in the mountains. I get so excited
everyday about going snowboarding,
whether it's a bad weather day and I'm
just hanging out with friends or it's the
most amazing powder day and the
pipes are perfect.'

BEAUTY SPOT

UV radiation can be up to 80 per cent higher on the mountain than it is at
lower altitudes. To avoid damaging your skin, regularly apply, and reapply,
a sun cream and lipsalve with a high sun protection factor (SPF). Get one
that's specifically formulated for the mountain and carry travel-size tubes
in your pocket or backpack.

GEAR

SNOWBOARD ANATOMY

There are different types of snowboard to suit different kinds of terrain and snow conditions, as well as styles of riding. However, they all have the same basic ingredients.

Nose The front end of the board.

Tail The back end of the board. You can usually distinguish the front and back ends of the board by looking at the graphics.

Edges The metal edges that surround the board. When you apply pressure to the edges they grip into the snow. These are your brakes.

Bindings You attach your feet to the board with bindings. These are usually mounted on the board with four screws that screw into holes called inserts. You can adjust the angle of your binds to set your stance. Bindings can loosen and so may need to be tightened regularly with a screwdriver or snowboard tool.

Leash A safety strap designed to stop your board running away from you. You can attach it to a lace hole on your boots.

Toe edge The edge nearest your toes; also known as the toeside or frontside.

Heel edge The edge nearest your heels; also known as the heelside or backside.

Width The width of your board. Different widths suit different sizes of feet and riders. Ideally, your feet should sit within the width of the board, although in some cases they may hang over – if you're unsure, ask for advice at a snowboard-specific store.

Sidecut Snowboards are narrower in the middle than they are at the nose and tail, creating a curve that allows the board to turn. A deep sidecut gives sharp turns; a shallow sidecut gives soft turns.

Flex The amount a board will bend. A board with plenty of flex across its width (torsional flex) will be easy to steer. A board with plenty of flex along its length (tip-to-tail flex) will make sharper turns. (See also Pop, below.)

Base The base of a snowboard is made from sintered polyethylene plastic, which sails over snow. When you ease off the edges and put more pressure on the base of the board you accelerate.

POP

Pop is the amount of spring your board has when you perform a trick like an *ollie*. A board with plenty of pop, or flex, is springy and elastic.

TYPES OF SNOWBOARDS

Freeride boards are relatively long with a deep sidecut, making them more stable at speed than freestyle boards. They can make sharp turns and have a *directional* shape. This means the nose is smaller than the tail and the board is designed to be ridden in one direction. Freeride boards also have a relatively stiff flex.

You can buy *freestyle boards* specifically designed for the halfpipe or rail, but most freestyle boards can handle a wider variety of obstacles and tricks. They're usually shorter, lighter, wider and more manoeuvrable than freeride boards and have *bi-directional* twin tips where the nose (or tip) and the tail are the same shape. This gives them the same feel whether you're riding forwards or backwards. They have a softer flex than freeride boards.

All mountain boards are a melding of the two board types and are designed to be ridden everywhere from off-piste to the halfpipe. This is the kind of board that you'll probably buy to begin with. If you're not sure what you're looking for, though, don't be afraid to ask.

97

There are now plenty of *women-specific boards* available which are designed to complement the female physique. They tend to be narrower and lighter making them more responsive for riders with less muscle and weight.

SIZING
When you stand your snowboard next to you it should come somewhere between your chin and your eyes. Snowboard lengths are measured in centimetres; for instance, someone who is 5'4" will probably want a board between 147- and 152-centimetres long. Remember: the shorter the board, the easier it will be to turn and the easier it will be to do tricks. The longer the board, the more stable it will be at speed.

SNOWBOARD TLC

Look after your board and get the base waxed and the edges sharpened regularly. You can do this yourself, but it's quicker and easier at this stage to leave it to the professionals. Do get someone to show you how to wax your board, though, as it's fairly easy with the right equipment and will quickly save you money. At the end of the season, you should apply wax to the bottom of your board before storing it – make sure you leave the board to dry out first.

BOOTS
In general, soft *freestyle* boots are more forgiving and therefore more popular than hard *Alpine boots*. What's most important, though, is that your boots fit properly and are comfortable so that you don't get foot cramp or pain. Try on as many boots and brands as you can. Different brands suit different feet. Always buy boots that fit your smallest foot – your toes should be just touching the ends when you stand up. The boots will stretch and ease off after a couple of wears. A boot with both an inner and external lacing system will keep movement to a minimum and will support your ankles. Make sure you're happy with the lace up

system and are able to do the boots up as tightly as you were shown in the shop. If you buy higher-end boots the inner linings can often be heat moulded for a custom fit, which is worth the time and effort.

BINDINGS
There are three types of binding systems – step in, flow and strap in. With *step-in* bindings the middle of the boot is connected to a binding plate on the snowboard and they are designed to be easy to take on and off. Avoid these at all times. This system allows lots of movement between the foot and board, leaking energy and reducing the responsiveness of the board.

The *flow* system has a soft material top that allows you to slip your boot into the bindings. These bindings are a better compromise than step-ins for beginners who want to be able to get their foot in and out of the bindings easily but they will gradually loosen and become less responsive.

The most responsive system is the traditional *strap-in* ratchet binding. Strap-ins take a bit of getting used to, but they're the best for performance and will last years. Both flow and strap-in bindings have *highbacks* that extend from the heel to lower calf; you can lean into these to control the heel edge of your board.

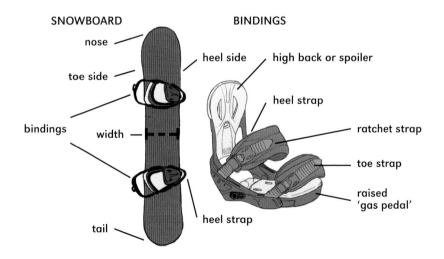

BINDING ANGLES

The angles at which your bindings are fixed to your board will affect your stance (see p103). You generally want a duck stance in which your back foot is angled slightly backwards. Front and back bindings are usually set about 25 to 30 degrees apart. A typical beginner stance would be -6 for the back foot and +18 or +21 for the front foot. Ask your instructor to check your binding angles and stance as it's easy to get it wrong.

PROTECTIVE GEAR

Wrist guards Wrist injuries are the most common type of injuries among snowboarders. Reduce the risk with a pair of wrist guards.

Goggles Steer clear of sunglasses which can easily come off and break, and only work in bright sunshine. Instead, invest in a pair of goggles with UV protection. These will keep out the wind and snow, and will help you see where you're going in a white out.

Helmet A snowboarding helmet is essential. Choose one which offers ventilation and, if you like listening to your favourite tunes on your iPod while you ride, get one that's compatible with an audio system. If you don't want to buy one initially, then you can hire helmets cheaply at resorts.

Body armour Though not essential, if you think that added padding will give you more confidence, protective body armour such as a *back protector* and *impact shorts* can be worn underneath your jacket and trousers.

CLOTHING

A well-fitting pair of waterproof *gloves* or *mitts* (warmer than gloves) with high cuffs will keep out the snow. If you feel the cold, wear an extra pair of glove liners and carry a hot gel hand warmer in your pocket.

Hat You lose around 80 per cent of your body heat through your head. Wear a tight-knit beanie beneath your helmet.

Waterproof jacket and trousers Don't go on the mountain without them. You can spend a fortune on outerwear, but as long as it has a waterproof level of 10,000 millimetres then you can buy low-end gear that works just as well.

Make sure your jacket and trousers fit comfortably over layers and are loose enough to allow you plenty of movement. Underarm, chest and thigh vents will help prevent you from getting too hot and sticky, while a high hood, powder skirt and Velcro cuffs on your jacket, and ankle gaiters on your trousers will keep out the snow.

Socks Warm tootsies are happy tootsies. Buy enough ski socks to last you the week. Always buy proper thermal ski socks from outdoor shops – your ordinary socks won't give you enough protection from the cold. Never double up on socks in your boots as this can give you cramps.

Layers Wear thermal base layers underneath a fleecy mid-layer so you can dress and undress according to the conditions. No matter how warm it is, however, never go boarding in just a T-shirt. Always wear at least a lightweight waterproof outer layer to shield you from sun- and snowburn.

Daypack A simple daypack is great for keeping essential items such as water, sunscreen, lipsalve, glove liners and energy snacks to hand.

BASIC TECHNIQUES

WARM UP
Warm up with a few star jumps or a bit of a run around before stretching out your whole body. This will help prevent injury if you take a tumble.

REGULAR OR GOOFY?
As with surfing, you need to know which foot you lead with. To work out whether you're goofy or regular, get a friend to give you a gentle shove from behind. If you

naturally step forward with your right foot, you're goofy; if you step forward with your left foot, you're regular.

STRAPPING IN

Find a quiet, flat area of the slope. Lie your board on the snow with the bindings down so that it doesn't run away. Now, crouch and turn the board towards you. Place your front foot (right if you're goofy, left if you're regular) in the front binding. Push your heel into the back of the binding, fasten the ankle strap, and then the toe strap. Attach the safety leash to your boot. Your binding should feel comfortably snug, not too tight. Now strap in your back foot. When both feet are strapped in there shouldn't be any movement between your foot, boot, binding or board.

STANCE

To find the basic stance, stand with your feet slightly wider than hip width apart. Hips should be relaxed and open. Tune into your centre of gravity just below your belly button and check your shoulders and upper body are in line with your hips. Now practise flexing your knees and extending up through your body. This flexion and extension creates natural suspension and helps you maintain balance.

Keep your arms relaxed by your side. Eyes are fixed on the horizon; don't look up or down or you'll fall over. Only your head should move when you want to change direction. Do not twist or turn your body. Roll onto the outside edges of your feet and practise applying pressure to the nose and then the tail of your board. This is how you steer your board.

GETTING UP

Firstly, make sure your board is pointing across the slope. Then, to get up onto the toeside, put your hands out in front of you, dig in with the toe edge and push up to standing through a squat. To get up onto the heelside from sitting, dig the heel edge into the slope and then push up with one arm and use the other for balance, until you come to standing. Keep an even pressure across your feet as you get up. If you're on your heelside and find it easier to get up on your toeside, switch edges (see p105).

SKATING AND STRAIGHT RUNNING

On the flat, strap your front foot into your binding. When you're ready, bring your back foot forward on the toeside, push off the snow and propel yourself forward. *Skating* is a bit like skateboarding, only it looks more awkward. Nevertheless, it's an easy way to get from A to B on the flat and is vital for negotiating lifts. Confident with that? Now place your back foot just in front of the back binding on the board and try *straight running*. Practise on the flat, then with your board facing down the fall line of a slight gradient. Apply pressure to the front of the board to speed up, to the back of the board to slow down.

FALLING DOWN

Avoid faceplants by anticipating falls. As soon as you feel yourself going, crouch down, cross your arms over your chest and fall softly onto your back. Now, get up, brush yourself off and try again!

FALL LINE

The *fall line* is the most direct path down a slope. If you dropped a ball on the snow at the top of a slope, it would roll down the fall line.

SIDE-SLIP

With your board pointing across a very gentle slope so that it cuts horizontally across the fall line, you can side-slip down a slope on either the toe or heel edge.

First, get up on your heelside and dig the edge into the snow so that you're in a stable, stationary position. Check your stance is relaxed and centred. Now, slowly bring the pressure in your heels forward towards your toes, so that the base of the board comes into contact with the snow. You will start moving down the slope. Lift up through your knees into an upright position to maintain balance. Look straight ahead. To stop, transfer the pressure back into your heels and dig the heel edge into the snow. As you practise, think of a 'pedalling' action. You apply pressure to your toes to accelerate, to your heels to slow down.

Now, switch sides. The toe edge can seem really scary as you're about to go down the slope backwards. Stand up on your toeside. Dig the toe edge into the snow, flexing your knees to keep your balance centred. Slowly take the pressure off your toes, moving it ever so slightly towards the heels. As the base of the board comes into contact with the snow you will start moving down the slope. Extend up through your body to maintain balance. Look straight ahead. Bring the pressure back into your toes when you want to slow down or stop. Remember that pedalling action.

DIAGONAL SIDE-SLIP
Start with the basic side-slip and then apply gentle pressure through your front foot towards the nose of the board so that you start moving in a diagonal direction across the slope. Apply opposing pressure to the outside edge of your back foot to maintain control. Turn your head (not your body!) in the direction you want to go. Practise this on the heelside, then the toeside.

SWITCHING EDGES

To practise toe- and heelside manoeuvres, rather than unstrapping your bindings, you can switch edges by rolling over in the snow. This will feel strange and clumsy at first.

FALLING LEAF
Falling leaf is a way of linking diagonal side-slips to get you used to controlling your direction. Practise on the heelside, then switch to the toeside.

From a side-slip, go into a diagonal side-slip, controlling your direction with pressure through the front foot. Stop. Now steer your board into a side-slip in the opposite direction, again taking it into a diagonal side-slip. This time control your direction with your back foot, which has now become your front foot. Repeat, mimicking the zigzag pattern of a falling leaf as you glide down the mountain.

GARLANDS

Again, *garlands* (so-called because it creates a pattern in the snow that looks like the garlands on a Christmas tree) is done on either the heel- or the toeside.

From the starting position with your board pointing across the slope, go into a side-slip and then diagonal side-slip. Now use your front foot to steer your board towards the direction of the fall line. Once the board starts to follow the fall line, steer it back across the slope and back into a side-slip. Stop in the starting position. Repeat. Practise until you can do this without stopping in-between.

TURNING

Once you can flow smoothly down the slope with garlands, you can start to think about your first turns. Begin with a simple C-shape turn. Get into the starting position for a side-slip. Go into a gentle side-slip and then steer your board into a diagonal side-slip. Increase the pressure in your feet until the board starts to turn down the slope. You will start to speed up as the board drops towards the fall line. Don't panic! Stay relaxed and committed and it will eventually cross the fall line as you switch edges. First turn completed, stop. Go back and practise this on both edges until you're confident enough to start linking the turns. Then, as you go from, say, toeside to heelside, heelside to toeside linking two turns, imagine that you are tracing an S-shape track in the snow.

FREESTYLE

Now it's time to add some style. There are three key techniques in freestyle – ollies, kickers and grabs. These provide the foundation for numerous other spectacular tricks (which all have confusing names that you'll soon pick up). But, they're not just confined to the parks and you'll see them being used elsewhere on the mountain.

An *ollie* is a jump from the flat that can be used for getting over small obstacles on the slopes and will come in handy when you start to make bigger jumps.

Here's how:

1 Begin straight running on a gentle slope.
2 Crouch down on your board and transfer pressure from the front to the back of your board. Use the tail of the board as a spring as you lift the nose of your board into the air.
3 Once the front foot is in the air, bring your knees up at a wide angle and level off the board.
4 Land on both feet, with knees and body relaxed to absorb the impact. Continue riding in a straight line.
5 Repeat until you've nailed it.

Girls who... Snowboard

Ruth Martin, 30, Action Sports
Marketing Consultant

'I'm not a naturally gifted athlete so every step of my journey in snowboarding has involved persistence. I'm now a decent enough snowboarder and ride well enough to go on cool backcountry journeys to beautiful places far from the piste. There's been great moments of freedom when I've just enjoyed the sheer exhilaration of snowboarding without feeling fear and without worrying about my ability.'

A *kicker* is a man-made or natural jump with a take off and a landing. As you approach the kicker, go into an ollie. Launch yourself off the kicker and then bring the board level in the air, as with an ollie. As you land, extend your legs slightly towards the ground. Flex your knees to absorb the impact.

Now go for a *grab*, which is exactly what it says on the tin. Jump off a kicker and grab your board in midair (at the nose, tail or in between your feet on either edge), tweaking the jump out to its most stylish point. Try a simple Indy grab first: grab your board on the toeside just in front of your back foot.

TAKING IT FURTHER
As your snowboarding progresses, you'll soon be eager to learn new skills and tricks. On the slopes, or maybe even off-piste, pick up some *speed* and start aiming to *carve*, cutting a thin groove in the snow with your edge as you turn. In the park, try jumps with *turns* such as the backside 180 or 360, have a go at riding the *rails* and, once you can ride backwards, known as *switch* or *fakie*, then you can take your first drop into the *halfpipe*.

SNOWBOARD FIT

CROSS-TRAINING
Get into a habit of doing 20 to 40 minutes of cardiovascular training such as running or swimming three times a week before you hit the slopes, increasing the intensity by adding intervals (periods of high intensity alternated with periods of low intensity) to your sessions.

Cycling and mountain biking are excellent cross-training for snowboarding as they'll boost both your cardiovascular fitness and your leg strength. Mountain biking on uneven terrain also works your core muscles and develops balance, both of which are essential in snowboarding. (For more tips on mountain biking, see p56.)

Also in the off-season include the Brazilian martial art dance capoeira, break dancing or b-bop, and gymnastics. These are especially good for improving your freestyle riding.

STRENGTH TRAINING

Squats, lunges, dead lifts and heel and toe raises are key strength exercises for snowboarding. However, it's a good idea to incorporate a few others as you will need strong arms for carrying your board and getting up, as well as a strong core for holding your stance. Try back extensions, tricep dips, press ups and core strength exercises such as the plank.

FLEXIBILITY

Both yoga and Pilates will help you develop balance, flexibility and core strength. Yoga can also help your mental focus giving you the confidence and commitment to take your snowboarding to the next level. Why not start the mornings in your chalet with a simple sun salutation and five minutes of meditation (see p139).

SNOWBOARD TRAVEL

DECIDING WHERE AND WHEN TO GO

The Austrian, French and Swiss Alps and the Canadian Rockies have some of the best snowboarding in the world (season: December to April). Famous resorts include Morzine, France, and Whistler, British Columbia. But there's also amazing snowboarding in the USA (season: November to June) and New Zealand (season: June to October). So, if you're prepared to travel, you could snowboard all year round. Try to avoid school holidays if you can as the resorts tend to be busiest around these times.

The nightlife at snow resorts can be legendary, especially if there's a festival or competition happening. If a wild après snow scene appeals, then go for a rowdier resort. If you want to be the first on the slopes in the morning, then think about opting for one where there's less temptation to stay out partying all night.

TRAVELLING BY PLANE

When booking your flight, check the airline's policy on carrying sports equipment as this can add a lot to the cost of your ticket. Pre-booking your board on a flight will often save you money. Find out about transfers to the resort before you arrive.

PACKING YOUR KIT

If you own a snowboard, buy a board bag – make sure you get one with padding to protect the board and a good strap so that it's easy to carry. Always remove your bindings from your board when you're travelling. You can then fill your board bag with all of your other gear, as well as extra clothes. Pack goggles in your hand luggage.

TOP FIVE PLACES TO SNOWBOARD...

...in Europe
Morzine/Avoriaz, French Alps
Val d'Isere, French Alps
Verbier, Swiss Alps
Cervinia-Zermatt, Austrian Alps
Crans Montana, Swiss Alps

...worldwide
Whistler, British Columbia, Canada
Mammoth, California, USA
New Zealand
Lake Tahoe, Nevada, USA
Vail, Colorado, USA

FIND OUT MORE

www.snowboardclub.co.uk Online home for the Snowboard Club UK.
www.powderroom.net Online women's snowboarding magazine.
www.snowboard.com Online snowboarding magazine and community.

IF YOU LIKE SNOWBOARDING, TRY...
Skiing
Mountain boarding
Skateboarding

JARGON BUSTER
Big air Big jump
Boardercross Competition event in which four to six snowboarders race each other down an obstacle course
Carve To turn, leaving clean arcs in the snow produced from good board performance and a high edge angle

Couloir A deep, steep gulley

Gnarly Nasty conditions or difficult terrain

Pow Powder; freshly fallen snow

Slalom and Giant Slalom Downhill racing events in which snowboarders carve their way between sets of poles known as gates

Slopestyle Snowboard competition in which the rider chooses their own route down a course with obstacles such as kickers, bumps and rails. They are judged on the difficulty and style of each trick

Snowpack The layers of snow that have built up throughout the season

Switch/fakie Riding your board backwards.

05

THE GIRL'S GUIDE TO
SURFING

WHAT IS IT?

Surfing is riding waves while balancing on a surfboard that has been designed to glide smoothly over the surface of the breaking water. There are two main types of surfboards and styles of surfing – longboarding (relaxed and chilled) and shortboarding (fast and feisty). Surfing can take a lifetime to perfect but, no matter what your level of experience, simply being in the ocean and harnessing the power of even the smallest wave for your own amusement is one of the best feelings in the world.

HOW IT ALL BEGAN

The first European record of surfing dates back to 1779 and was written by James King, first lieutenant of Captain Cook's ship *Discovery*. In his log book King describes how the locals at Kealakekua Bay on the Pacific Island of Hawaii braved the swell on huge planks of wood, flying at great speed on the crest of a wave before diving beneath the surface to avoid their craft as the surf came crashing down on the rocks and the beach.

Although little is known about the early history of the Polynesians, there's no doubt that by the late 1700s surfing was ingrained in the culture of these great watermen and women. Sadly, however, the arrival of the white-skinned Westerners heralded a period of decline of surfing and traditional island culture, and many Hawaiians were wiped out by diseases, alcohol and other foreign ills.

Yet the allure of surfing could not be lost forever. Much of its revival is credited to the writer Jack London, who visited Hawaii in the early 1900s. London subsequently wrote 'A Royal Sport: Surfing in Waikiki', which made surfing famous in the USA. It was thanks to Hawaiian beach boy Duke Paoa Kahanamoku, however, that surfing gained recognition on other continents. An Olympic swimmer who travelled widely, Duke demonstrated surfing wherever he went.

Although surfing has been a largely male-dominated sport in its modern history, an increasing number of women can now been seen in the lineup, their grace, fluidity and style an inspiration to *wahines* (female surfers) the world over – from San Sebastian in Northern Spain to San Diego in Southern California.

BODY AND MIND BENEFITS

Surfing sculpts your arms, shoulders and back muscles, and torso. It also works your legs since, beginners especially, spend a lot of time messing around and wading about in the *white water* (the broken water near the shoreline). But, since you'll be so concentrated on catching those waves, you won't even notice you're doing exercise!

Like all physical activity, surfing releases happy hormones called endorphins, which make you feel positive and motivated. And there are other psychological benefits too – increased confidence, and improved focus and awareness, concentration, patience and tenacity. On a spiritual level, surfing can inspire feelings of humility as it teaches you to respect the sea, nature and others around you.

Girls who... Surf

Pearl Howie, 35, Communications
Professional

*'Knowing that I have the confidence
to get out there and surf makes me
feel more confident in other areas of
my life. Knowing that I've tried
something new and loved it, makes
me feel more positive about trying
other new things too. Even if I'm not
the best surfer, I'm in my element on
the beach and that feeling carries
over, even back to the city.'*

GETTING STARTED

SURF STYLE

Surfing largely falls into two categories: *long boarding* and *short boarding*, which not only differ in the shape and size of boards, but also in the waves you'll ride and the style in which you surf.

A longboard is usually around nine feet long, and is fat and wide. Although it's possible to take on bigger surf, longboards are better suited to smaller, friendlier waves. You can take a longboard out even in tiny surf and you're guaranteed to have fun. The riding style is chilled out and you'll see longboarders performing

117

dance-like moves on the board as they *trim* along a wave. Shortboards are much neater, measuring in at under seven feet long, and are slim and light enough to hook easily under your arm and carry to the beach. Shortboards like big, powerful waves, which makes everything much faster and meaner.

For beginners, however, the most important thing is not what board or style you ride, but simply to get out there and have fun. For this reason, your first surf experiences will probably be on a Mini-Mal, which is somewhere between a longboard and shortboard. Rent one to begin with, then think about buying your own.

YOUR FIRST SURFBOARD

Once you're ready to make the investment, choose carefully. Go to a specialist surf shop and ask lots of questions until you find something you like. Tell the assistant your height and weight, so they can help you choose a board that's right for you; later you can think about having a board custom-made to your measurements and surfing style.

Make sure the board fits easily under you arm. You don't want to get lumped with something that's literally a pain to carry down to the beach. You may want to try out a women-specific board too.

Buying secondhand or ex-rental is an option. Just make sure there's not any major damage to the board, such as cracks, creases or delamination, and take a knowledgeable friend with you when you go to look at the board.

SURF SCIENCE

As long as the waves aren't too big and the weather isn't too wild, the conditions are fairly irrelevant at this stage as you just need to get out and practise whatever the surf is like. However, it's never too early to start learning a bit about how to predict the surf conditions at your local break. Here's what you need to know.

Waves are created by wind rubbing against the surface of the water. This can happen close to the coast, in which case the waves generated are called *windswell*. On rare occasions this can produce rideable surf, but what you're really after is *groundswell*. Groundswell comes from far out at sea. When there's a storm over the ocean, the waves it makes gradually organise themselves into *sets*. By the time these reach the coast, the waves will have gained in momentum and energy, finally giving rise to surf as they break on or near the shore.

Keep an eye on the *weather charts* and you'll soon be able to recognise where there's a storm brewing in the ocean, how powerful the subsequent *swell* might be and when it's likely to arrive at a surf spot near you. Look for *isobars* (thin squiggly lines with numbers indicating pressure) circulating around a central area of low pressure, known as a *depression* or *low*. The isobars also more or less mark air movement and the closer they are together the bigger and stronger the waves are likely to be.

Next it's helpful to look at the *buoy charts*. These show *swell direction* along with *wave height* and *wave period*. The wave height is the height of the wave from *peak* (top) to *trough* (bottom) as it travels through the ocean – for a rough indication of what size the waves will be at the shore, look at the wave height at buoys near your break. While more experienced surfers get excited about the prospect of a big swell, you're best off sticking to the smaller days for now. Ideally, you want a wave about one- to three-feet high. Sounds tiny, but even waves that appear small from the shore can feel huge close up. You'll hear waves described as *waist-high, shoulder-high* or *head-high*. If a wave is *double overhead*, it's twice head-high. If it's *triple overhead*, run for your life!

Meanwhile, the wave period is the time in seconds between two waves as they pass the buoy. Generally, the longer the wave period, the further it has travelled, and the more organised the swell will be by the time it reaches the coast. Swell that has travelled a long way is called long-range swell and has the potential to produce really well-formed surf.

Another factor affecting the shape of the surf is the wind. So, look at a map and work out what direction a particular *break* is facing. Then, go back to the weather charts and find out what direction and speed the *winds* will be travelling. If the wind is heading directly from the sea towards the coast, it's called *onshore*. This is bad, as it means *messy* waves and the surf will be a soup of white water. If the wind is heading in the opposite direction, from the coast towards the sea, then it's called *offshore*. This is good, as it can mean perfectly formed waves with plenty of clean, green water to ride. If the wind is travelling diagonally in either direction, then it's called *cross-shore*, and the conditions may be hit or miss. As far as wind speed goes, you don't want anything with too much force. A light to moderate wind is ideal. Alternatively, head for a more *sheltered* break or plan a sunrise or sunset surf when winds on the coast tend to drop, the air is calm and still, and the waves *clean* and *glassy*.

The final thing to consider is the *tide*. Tides are created by the effect of the moon's force on the ocean surface, which causes the water to rise and fall. As well as concealing or revealing rocks, tides can also have a huge impact on the shape and force of waves. Some breaks may look flat on a low tide, but come alive at high tide. Whether the tide is rising (coming in; you'll hear people say it's "on the push"), *falling* (going out) or *on the turn* (switching; changing direction) can also have an effect. If you're lucky enough to live near the ocean, learn how your nearby breaks respond. Otherwise, ask a local. You can usually pick up a *tide chart* at surf shops, which will give you the times for high and low tides, and sunrise and sunset too.

SURF REPORTS

There are plenty of handy surf report websites on the internet that do all the hard work for you and, although they don't always get it right, they transform complex meteorological data into simple star ratings. Many also feature webcams or links to local webcams so, if you can't get down there yourself, you can see what's going on at the beach.

BREAKS

When a wave hits a sandbar on the bottom on the sea bed, forcing it to break, it's called a *beachbreak*. But sand shifts all the time, so a beachbreak can be unpredictable. If there's a sandbank close to the shore, it can produce a steep, hollow wave ideal for shortboarding. Beginners should stay clear of these, however, as they have a habit of dumping you onto the hard sand. Instead, look for beachbreaks where the sandbanks are producing a more manageable wave further from the shore.

When the coastline bends or juts out at an angle it can create a *pointbreak*. Waves break more consistently than at a beachbreak and peel, one after the other, towards the shore. Find a good one, and you'll be in beginner's surf heaven. A *reefbreak* on the other hand, can be beginner's hell. This is where a wave breaks over a reef or rocks. The waves break consistently in the same place and have a consistent shape. But the seabed below is hard and often sharp. Save reefbreaks for later.

WAVE SHAPES
A *mushy* wave breaks gradually and gently, with little power behind it and is fine for beginners. A wave with more shape may start to *peel* as it breaks – these types of waves are sublime. Less appealing, though, is a *closeout*, where the wave breaks in one long, messy line. A *hollow* wave is one that forms a *barrel* or *tube* as it breaks. This is caused when the wave suddenly goes from deep water to shallow water, often over a reef. Riding a hollow wave, or *getting barrelled*, is a surfer's dream.

LEFTS AND RIGHTS
If you're on a wave, looking towards the beach, and the wave is breaking to your right and you are riding it to the right, it's called a *right* or *righthander*. If it's breaking to your left and you are riding it to the left, it's a *left* or *lefthander*. You'll soon develop a preference for one or the other.

RIPS
Rips, or *currents*, are formed over channels that are deeper than the rest of the seabed and which present the easiest way for the water to flow back out to sea after it's hit the shore. Rips aren't always immediately obvious, but you can spot them if you look carefully: the giveaway is a section of choppy water where the waves are refusing to break. Rips can be a surfer's friend or foe. More experienced surfers often use them to get out to the *lineup*, the point just behind

where the surf breaks where you wait to catch the waves. However, some rips can be lethal, whisking you out to sea at a frightening speed.

ESCAPING A RIP

If you get caught in a rip, don't panic. Stay calm and paddle *across* the rip and you'll eventually get out. Paddling against the rip is futile and will only drain you of valuable energy.

GEAR GUIDE

SURFBOARDS
Longboard Longboards are nine feet or more in length and are thick and wide, with a round *nose* and wide *tail*. They're easy to paddle, buoyant and stable.

Shortboard Coming in at under seven feet, shortboards are thin and narrow, with a pointed nose and a pintail. They're less stable but more manoeuvrable than a longboard.

Mini-Mal These measure around 7-8 feet, have many of the stable, buoyant characteristics of a longboard, but are slightly narrower and thinner and have a more pointed nose, so they'll give you a taste of what it's like to ride a shortboard. They're perfect for beginners.

Foamboard Many people learn to surf on a foam board. These are a similar length to a Mini-Mal, but are made of thick foam and have soft fins. This means no bumps, no bruises and you'll be able to catch even the smallest wave or puff of white water.

Softboard A step up from a foam board is a softboard or *surface board*. It has a smooth bottom (so it will glide through the water more easily than a foam

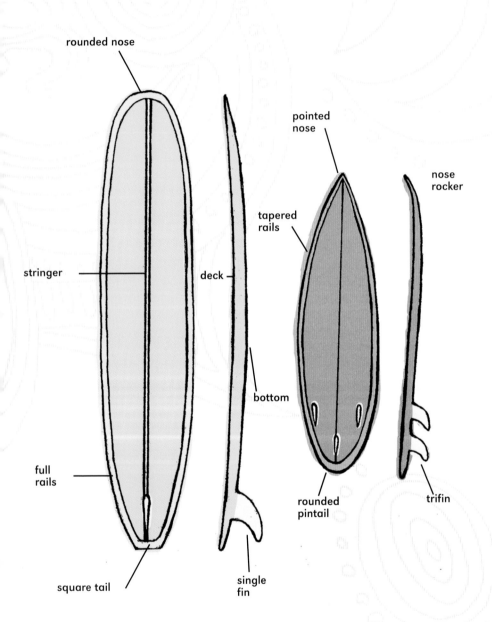

MINI-MAL

SHORTBOARD

rounded nose

stringer

full
rails

square tail

deck

bottom

single
fin

pointed
nose

tapered
rails

rounded
pintail

nose
rocker

trifin

board), a soft compact foam top and soft fins (so, again, no bumps and bruises). It's more manoeuvrable than a foam board and will allow you start practising turns.

Other types of surfboards Beyond the boards mentioned above, there's the *fish*, a short, stocky board that's designed for shortboarders who want to ride small waves, and the *gun*, or *rhino chaser*, a narrow board that's seven-plus feet long and is designed for big-wave riding. Make sure you don't mistake a gun for a Mini-Mal when you're buying your first board.

Surfboard anatomy As you've learnt you can buy all sorts of different surfboards. However, they all have the same basic ingredients.

Dimensions The dimensions, or *specifications*, are written somewhere on the board, either on the deck or on the bottom. Measured in feet and inches, they refer to the length, nose width, middle width and thickness of your board.

Volume The volume of the board refers to how much foam is used to make the inner board. More foam gives more buoyancy and stability. Beginners and heavier surfers need plenty of volume.

Foil The foil is the distribution of volume, which should be greatest underneath your chest, gradually tapering out towards the nose and tail.

Rails The edges of the surfboard are called the rails. The harder and sharper your rails, the faster and tighter your board will turn. Soft, rounded (or *full*) rails are best for beginners as the board will be more stable.

Rocker The rocker is the curve of your board. It affects your ability to turn, as well as your speed. You can have a rocker at both the nose and the tail. The bigger the rocker, the easier your board will be to turn.

Bottom There are different types of board bottom, such as vee, channel and concave. Beginners should look for something fairly flat or slightly convex.

Deck The deck of the board is the top of the board on which you stand. Flat decks are the most buoyant and stable, domed decks are found on performance boards.

Stringer The stringer is a thin piece of wood running through the centre of the board from nose to tail to give the board strength and flexibility. Bigger boards can have up to three stringers.

Tail Different tails are designed for different surf conditions – there's the narrow *pintail* for big, steep surf; the *squaretail* for average conditions; and the *roundtail*, which is mid-way between the two and offers buoyancy as well as manoeuvrability.

Fins At the back of the board, you'll find the fins. These help you to drive and turn the board. Longboards usually have a *singlefin*, while shortboards usually have a *trifin*. Generally, the bigger the fin, the more stability it will provide; the smaller the fin, the more manoeuvrability. Some fins are *glassed* into the board when it's made. More common are detachable *Fin Control Systems* (FCS), which you screw into your board with a *fin key*. Just make sure you've put the fins on the right way round.

LOOKING AFTER YOUR SURFBOARD

When you're not using your board, keep it out of the sun and tuck it safely away in a board bag. Never lean it against a wall or a car, as it can easily fall and crash to the floor. If you want to lie it down, then do so on top of your board bag or deckside down on the floor – scratch the bottom of the board and it will affect how it moves through the water. Don't place your board somewhere that someone might trip or drive over it. When carrying it around, watch you don't knock the nose, tail or rails on walls, steps or other people.

SURFBOARD ACCESSORIES

Leash A leash attaches you to your board. You fix one end of the leash to the plug at the tail end of your board and the other to the ankle of your back foot with a Velcro strap. Some ankle straps have a hidden pocket inside which you can stow your car key.

Wax and grip If you've any hope of staying put on your board, you'll need to create a sticky surface on its deck for your feet to grip. The traditional way of doing this is with *wax*. When you first get your new surfboard, apply a layer of base coat, followed by wax. The *base coat* will last a long time, but you'll need to reapply the wax from time to time or rough up the surface with a *wax comb*. There are different types of wax for different water temperatures – cold (below 14.5°C), cool (14.5 to 20°C), warm (20 to 25.5°C) and tropical (over 25.5°C). Look for non-toxic, eco-friendly waxes, which are often made from beeswax. Alternatively, you can use a *grip*, which is a permanent rubber pad that sticks to the back and/or front of your board where you place your feet.

WAX ON, WAX OFF

To wax your board...

- Generously apply a base coat in smooth, sweeping motions up and down the length of the board until you can see and feel little bobbles covering the board. This can take a bit of time and you'll probably use up a whole bar.
- Now repeat the process with a bar of wax, using small circular motions. Make sure it's the right wax for the water temperature.
- In the future, simply reapply the wax in places where it has worn thin or, if there's still a lot of wax on the board, rough it up with a wax comb.
- If your board starts to look dirty and you want to give it a new wax job, soften the wax by leaving your board in the sun. Scrape both the base coat and wax off using the smooth edge of the wax comb or an old credit card. Once it's clean, reapply the base coat and then the wax as you did before.

Board bag If you're really strapped for cash, get a terry towelling *sock*. Better though, is a reinforced foam-lined *board bag* that's made from reflective material and will help protect your board from the heat and elements.

Repair kit With the help of a ding repair kit, small *dings* (dents) are easy to fix. Take bigger dings to a professional; it'll cost you, but not as much as a new board.

BODY ACCESSORIES

Wetsuits The biggest expense after your surfboard, and worth every penny, is a *wetsuit*. Made from neoprene, wetsuits keep you warm by locking in an insulating layer of water between the wetsuit and your skin. For this reason, it's crucial your wetsuit fits well and has a watertight zip and sealed seams. Don't buy the first one you see, try on as many different brands and sizes as you can before you hand over hard-earned cash. (Never, ever go shopping for wetsuits on a hot, sticky day. Nightmare.)

You can buy a wetsuit for every season and water temperature. But you won't ever really need more than two – one for summer and one for winter. Go for a full-length suit each time. You could get a *shorty* with short arms and legs for summer, but it won't offer as much protection from the sun and you may as well wear a long-sleeved *rash vest* and *board shorts* if the water's that warm.

Wetsuit thickness is measured in millimetres and the material on the torso is always thicker than on the arms. For example, a winter suit designed for water temperatures between 4°C and 10°C will be described as a 5/3 (you say: 'five three'). A summer suit designed for water temperatures between 12°C and 18°C will be a 3/2 (you say: 'three two').

After every session, wash your wetsuit thoroughly in fresh water to flush out sea water and wee (no-one wants to cut short a good surf session just to pee). Hang it over a drying rack and leave to drip dry. Never put it in direct sunlight as this will ruin your wetsuit.

Hood, gloves and booties If you're intent on surfing through the winter months, then a *hood* and a pair of *gloves* and *booties* will all provide additional warmth to your wetsuit. Some people hate being cocooned in neoprene. But it all depends on your ability to tolerate the cold and if you're freezing cold within five minutes of getting in the water, it's not going to be much fun anyway.

Rash vest Made from neoprene or Lycra, a rash vest worn in warm water will keep off the wind and the sun, offering invaluable UV protection. It will also prevent you from getting a rash on your stomach and chest from rubbing against the board when you're paddling. Thermal rash vests that can be worn beneath your wetsuit have a gorgeous fleecy lining that add a touch of luxury to any winter surf session.

Bikini Surfing in your beach bikini won't win you any prizes. Your breasts will flop out and bikini bottoms can quickly become wedged between bum cheeks. Not a good look; may as well wear a thong. Buy a proper surf bikini with more support. And, especially if you're wearing a bikini underneath your wetsuit, avoid ones with string ties as these can get caught in the zip and the knots can be annoying.

Boardshorts Perhaps a safer bet than bikini bottoms, boardshorts are made from fast-drying material and, providing you get the right fit, look pretty cool. The women's versions now come in every length from ankle-slappers to three-quarter length, to hotpant-style. If you don't like girlie colours, try a pair of men's boardshorts for size.

Sun protection A long-sleeved rash vest and boardshorts offer more protection than a bikini, with a full-length wetsuit going one step better. Generously apply a water-resistant suncream with an SPF of 30-plus to any areas of skin that are left uncovered, including face, ears and hands. Don't forget to do this even on overcast or rainy days.

First aid kit Always carry a first aid kit with you in the back of your car. Buy a ready-made one from the chemist, or make up your own.

Plastic box or bag Keep a plastic box or bag in the back of your car for your wetsuit, damp towels and wet swimwear.

BEAUTY SPOT

It's not only your skin that is vulnerable to the sun, sea and wind. Your hair can take a battering too. Protect your locks with an oil or spray that offers UV protection or by simply combing suncream through your hair with your fingers. Wash your hair thoroughly after every surf and regularly restore moisture with an intensive conditioning treatment.

Girls who... Surf

Roslyn Cassidy, 49, Business Owner

'The water holds me and throws me around and spins me upside down and, occasionally, I catch a wave for one or two or 10 seconds and then I am truly happy and free... until I get dunked again. That's why I love surfing.'

BASIC TECHNIQUES

POPPING UP

The swift action that takes you from a flat-down paddling position on your board to standing is called a *pop up*. It should be done in one fast, smooth move and is something that will only come with practice. But, you don't need to be in the surf to do so. You can practise in your living room or on the beach.

THE POP UP

1   Lie (or imagine you are lying) on your board.
2   Place your hands beneath your chest and push up your upper body with straight arms.
3   Snap your legs up to standing, placing your feet a good hip-distance apart. Your front foot should land roughly where your chest was.
4   Bend your knees into a stable, half squat. No straight legs and don't stick your bum out! Front arm out, back elbow bent to counterbalance. Head and chest up, look in the direction you want to go.

GOOFY OR REGULAR?

When you practise your pop ups you'll notice that one foot naturally falls to the front. If it's your right foot, then you're *goofy*; if it's your left foot, you're *regular*. There's no right or wrong, and neither one is better than the other. Just remember which you are, as you always attach your leash to your back foot when you surf.

WARM-UP

Even if you're aching to get in the water, don't forget to warm up and do a few stretches before you surf. It will be much easier to paddle out and your pop ups will be much smoother. Take a gentle run up and down the beach to get the blood flowing, then do some simple stretches or yoga poses.

ATTACHING YOUR LEASH

The final thing you need to do before you get in the water is to attach your leash to the ankle of your back foot – if you prefer, you could attach it to your leg just below your knee. When you're carrying your board to or from the water, wrap it around the tail just behind the fins and secure it with the Velcro strap. When you're wading out, keep your board tucked under your arm and keep hold of the middle of your leash with your hand until the water is waist height. Then, let go of your leash and let it trail behind you as you paddle or wade out further.

PADDLING

Before you go for your first wave, practise paddling. You can do this even on a flat day. Lie on your board and make sure you're centred – not too far forward, not too far back – so the board is stable and you're able to slip through the water. Keep your feet and legs together and very slightly arch your back. Now paddle, driving your arms forward one after the other, just as you would if you were swimming front crawl. Slightly cup your hands, scoop them under the board, and then pull them back through the water.

CATCHING YOUR FIRST WAVE

Wade out to where the water is just above waist-high. When you see a wave coming, position the board so it's facing towards the beach and lie on it, making sure you're centred. As the wave approaches, start paddling. Keep paddling hard (harder! You want to have the same speed as the wave by the time it reaches you) until you feel the wave's momentum pick you up and magic-carpet you towards the shore. Practise this until you can confidently catch wave after wave. Then, start popping up. Pop up as soon as you feel the swoosh of being taken by the white water. As you get more confident, wade or paddle out a little further past the white water to catch the smaller, unbroken waves.

WIPING OUT

When you *wipe out*, or fall off your board, try to fall off the back or to one side. Curl your arms around your head to protect your head and then wait a few seconds before coming to the surface. If you're held underneath, don't panic, you'll soon surface. As soon as you come up, look around for your board and then quickly grab hold of it, using the leash to pull it towards you if you can't reach.

PADDLING OUT

Ready for the next challenge? Then it's time to make your way towards the lineup to catch some bigger unbroken waves. Don't worry if you don't get there the first time, paddling out is harder than it looks.

Once you've waded out as far as you can go, hop on your board and *punch through* the smaller, breaking waves. As the wave approaches, *push up* with your arms and let the water flow through the gap you have created between the board and your body. If the waves are too big to punch through, stop and wait until there is a *lull* between sets – make sure that you are not in the way of others who are up and riding. Then, when the lull arrives, paddle like crazy.

If you want to carry on paddling, though, or there is no real lull between sets, try a *turtle roll*. Just before the breaking wave reaches you, grab onto the rails, flip your board upside down and hold it parallel to your body, close to your chest. Once the wave has passed, flip back over onto the top of your board and carry on paddling. It's scary at first, but easy once you know how.

Another way of getting out is to *duck dive* your board through a wave. However, this is largely the preserve of shortboarders and is virtually impossible with a Mini-Mal or longboard.

If all else fails, your final option is to bail out. As the wave approaches, ditch your board and dive through the wave. As soon as you are through the wave, pull your board close to you, get back on and paddle, paddle, paddle. Avoid bailing out if there are other surfers nearby as you don't want to take them out with your flailing surfboard.

IN THE LINEUP

Once you've reached the lineup – well done! – take a breather. Position yourself roughly in line with the other surfers and sit up, straddling the centre of your board. Face towards the horizon, so that you can see the sets approaching. When you're rested and ready to catch a wave, wait your turn. Remember your surf etiquette (see p136). But, equally, don't be shy. Name your wave and go for it.

POSITIONING YOURSELF ON THE WAVE

As the wave approaches, whisk yourself around with your legs. Look over your shoulder to see which way the wave is breaking and position your board so you're gently angled in the same direction, just below the crest of the wave. Lie on your board and make sure you're centred – if you're too far forward you'll do a dramatic nose dive, if you're too far back you won't be able to catch the wave. Paddle as hard as you can then, as you feel the wave take you, do three more power paddles just to be sure, and pop up to your feet. Look down the wave in the direction you want to go, bend your knees, keep your bodyweight low and use your arms for balance.

TURNING

Once you've got used to catching waves, you can try some basic turns. By applying pressure to your back foot and to the inside (for a *bottom turn*) or outside (for a *top turn*) rails, you can steer the board. But, start by simply looking in the direction that you want to go. Where your gaze leads, your shoulders, your body and board will naturally follow.

TAKING IT FURTHER

Congratulations, you're surfing! But there's still so much to learn, so keep practising. Nominate a *mentor*, an experienced surfer who will push you and help you develop your technique. Have a go at longboarding, try *cross-stepping* down the board, go for a *nose-ride, hang five* or *ten* with your toes over the end of the board. Or switch to a shortboard to see how it feels.

SURF ETIQUETTE

Surfing's a laid back sport, but it does have a few simple rules:
- Surf in the white water or at a known beginner's spot until you are competent and confident enough to catch smaller unbroken waves or to take on more challenging breaks.

- Stay out of the way of other surfers when you're paddling out. If a set has come through and you're close to the shore, wait until all the waves have been caught before making your way back out to the lineup. If you're in the way of an oncoming surfer, stay put so they can surf around you.

- Pay attention to what is going on in the lineup and wait your turn. As a beginner, it may be best to go for the waves that other people miss, but don't use this an excuse to hold back.

- Try not to *drop in* on someone else's wave. The wave belongs to the person closest to where the wave breaks. This is called the *peak*. If someone else is up and riding, back off. Wait for the next wave.

- If you looked in both directions before you took off and were sure it was all clear, but find that you have accidentally dropped in on someone, don't fret, it happens. Pull back on your board, smile and apologise!

Girls who... Surf

Belinda Baggs, 28, Professional
Longboarder

*'If you think of surfing as a mere
sport, then give it up and play
tennis. If you love surfing and
feel it beating in your heart, then
it doesn't matter how good or
bad you are – just have fun, get
out there as often as you can
and pay attention to all good
advice.'*

SURF FIT

YOGA

Yoga develops strength, flexibility and balance, as well as mental clarity, all of which are essential for surfing. Regular practice can be hugely beneficial and help you to develop good technique, as well as help prevent muscle imbalances and potential injuries. Many people begin their yoga practice with a sun salutation, which is also a great way to warm up before your surf.